DISCARDED

Here's all the great literature in this grade level of *Celebrate Reading!*

Books A–D

EN GARDE !!

Make Way for
Sam Houston
JEAN
FRITZ
Illustrations
by Elise
Primavera

ODYSSEY
BASEBALL
IN APRIL
AND OTHER STORIES

GARY SOTO

LAURENCE YEP

The Star Fisher

If This Is Love
I'll Take Spaghetti

The Deciding Factor
Learning What Matters

Featured Poet
Gary Soto

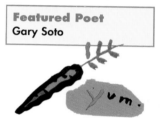

Book A Celebrate Reading!

A Volcano of Cheers

Chasing Your Goals

Book B Celebrate Reading!

The First Magnificent Web

Tales of the Imagination

Featured Poets
Jack Prelutsky
Lewis Carroll
Richard Armour
Eve Merriam

JABBERWOCKY

Aida
Leontyne Price

ILLUSTRATED BY
LEO AND DIANE DILLON

Book C Celebrate Reading!

A Better Time Slot

From There to Here

**More Great Books
to Read!**

The Grizzly
by Annabel and
Edgar Johnson

**Where the Lillies
Bloom**
by Vera and Bill Cleaver

The Master Puppeteer
by Katherine Paterson

**The Bread Sister of
Sinking Creek**
by Robin Moore

Maniac Magee
by Jerry Spinelli

Sweetwater
by Laurence Yep

It's Like This, Cat
by Emily Neville

Let the Hurricane Roar
by Rose Wilder Lane

THE DECIDING ★ FACTOR

Cover Artist
The paintings of Seth Jaben convey his personal philoso-
phy of humor and optimism. Mr. Jaben says that his art is
conceived to leave a trail of smiles and to inspire the pur-
suit of each person's dream.

ISBN: 0-673-80071-7

Acknowledgments appear on page 144.

678910RRS9998979695

THE DECIDING ★ FACTOR

LEARNING WHAT MATTERS

📖 ScottForesman

A Division of HarperCollins*Publishers*

CONTENTS

Gary Soto

SEVENTH GRADE

On the first day of school, Victor stood in line half an hour before he came to a wobbly card table. He was handed a packet of papers and a computer card on which he listed his one elective, French. He already spoke Spanish and English, but he thought some day he might travel to France, where it was cool; not like Fresno, where summer days reached 110 degrees in the shade. There were rivers in France, and huge churches, and fair-skinned people everywhere, the way there were brown people all around Victor.

Besides, Teresa, a girl he had liked since they were in catechism classes at Saint Theresa's, was taking French, too. With any luck they would be in the same class. Teresa is going to be my girl this year, he promised himself as he left the gym full of students in their new fall clothes.

She was cute. And good at math, too, Victor thought as he walked down the hall to his homeroom. He ran into his friend, Michael Torres, by the water fountain that never turned off.

They shook hands, *raza*-style, and jerked their heads at one another in a *saludo de vato*. "How come you're making a face?" asked Victor.

"I ain't making a face, *ese*. This *is* my face." Michael said his face had changed during the summer. He had read a *GQ* magazine that his older brother borrowed from the Book Mobile and noticed that the male models all had the same look on their faces. They would stand, one arm around a beautiful woman, and *scowl*. They would sit at a pool, their rippled stomachs dark with shadow, and *scowl*. They would sit at dinner tables, cool drinks in their hands, and *scowl*.

"I think it works," Michael said. He scowled and let his upper lip quiver. His teeth showed along with the ferocity of his soul. "Belinda Reyes walked by a while ago and looked at me," he said.

Victor didn't say anything, though he thought his friend looked pretty strange. They talked about recent movies, baseball, their parents, and the horrors of picking grapes in order to buy their fall clothes. Picking grapes was like living in Siberia, except hot and more boring.

"What classes are you taking?" Michael said, scowling.

"French. How 'bout you?"

"Spanish. I ain't so good at it, even if I'm Mexican."

"I'm not either, but I'm better at it than math, that's for sure."

A tinny, three-beat bell propelled students to

their homerooms. The two friends socked each other in the arm and went their ways, Victor thinking, man, that's weird. Michael thinks making a face makes him handsome.

On the way to his homeroom, Victor tried a scowl. He felt foolish, until out of the corner of his eye he saw a girl looking at him. Umm, he thought, maybe it does work. He scowled with greater conviction.

In homeroom, roll was taken, emergency cards were passed out, and they were given a bulletin to take home to their parents. The principal, Mr. Belton, spoke over the crackling loudspeaker, welcoming the students to a new year, new experiences, and new friendships. The students squirmed in their chairs and ignored him. They were anxious to go to first period. Victor sat calmly, thinking of Teresa, who sat two rows away, reading a paperback novel. This would be his lucky year. She was in his homeroom, and would probably be in his English and math classes. And, of course, French.

The bell rang for first period, and the students herded noisily through the door. Only Teresa lingered, talking with the homeroom teacher.

"So you think I should talk to Mrs. Gaines?" she asked the teacher. "She would know about ballet?"

"She would be a good bet," the teacher said. Then added, "Or the gym teacher, Mrs. Garza."

Victor lingered, keeping his head down and staring at his desk. He wanted to leave when she did so he could bump into her and say something clever.

He watched her on the sly. As she turned to

leave, he stood up and hurried to the door, where he managed to catch her eye. She smiled and said, "Hi, Victor."

He smiled back and said, "Yeah, that's me." His brown face blushed. Why hadn't he said, "Hi, Teresa," or "How was your summer?" or something nice?

As Teresa walked down the hall, Victor walked the other way, looking back, admiring how gracefully she walked, one foot in front of the other. So much for being in the same class, he thought. As he trudged to English, he practiced scowling.

In English they reviewed the parts of speech. Mr. Lucas, a portly man, waddled down the aisle, asking, "What is a noun?"

"A person, place, or thing," said the class in unison.

"Yes, now somebody give me an example of a person—you, Victor Rodriguez."

"Teresa," Victor said automatically. Some of the girls giggled. They knew he had a crush on Teresa. He felt himself blushing again.

"Correct," Mr. Lucas said. "Now provide me with a place."

Mr. Lucas called on a freckled kid who answered, "Teresa's house with a kitchen full of big brothers."

After English, Victor had math, his weakest subject. He sat in the back by the window, hoping that he would not be called on. Victor understood most of the problems, but some of the stuff looked like the teacher made it up as she went along. It was confusing, like the inside of a watch.

After math he had a fifteen-minute break, then social studies, and, finally, lunch. He bought a tuna casserole with buttered rolls, some fruit cocktail, and milk. He sat with Michael, who practiced scowling between bites.

Girls walked by and looked at him.

"See what I mean, Vic?" Michael scowled. "They love it."

"Yeah, I guess so."

They ate slowly, Victor scanning the horizon for a glimpse of Teresa. He didn't see her. She must have brought lunch, he thought, and is eating outside. Victor scraped his plate and left Michael, who was busy scowling at a girl two tables away.

The small, triangle-shaped campus bustled with students talking about their new classes. Everyone was in a sunny mood. Victor hurried to the bag lunch area, where he sat down and opened his math book. He moved his lips as if he were reading, but his mind was somewhere else. He raised his eyes slowly and looked around. No Teresa.

He lowered his eyes, pretending to study, then looked slowly to the left. No Teresa. He turned a page in the book and stared at some math problems that scared him because he knew he would have to do them eventually. He looked to the right. Still no sign of her. He stretched out lazily in an attempt to disguise his snooping.

hen he saw her. She was sitting with a girlfriend under a plum tree. Victor moved to a table near her and daydreamed about taking her to a movie. When the bell sounded, Teresa looked up, and their eyes met. She smiled sweetly and gathered her books. Her next class was French, same as Victor's.

They were among the last students to arrive in class, so all the good desks in the back had already been taken. Victor was forced to sit near the front, a few desks away from Teresa, while Mr. Bueller wrote French words on the chalkboard. The bell rang, and Mr. Bueller wiped his hands, turned to the class, and said, *"Bonjour."*

"Bonjour," braved a few students.

"Bonjour," Victor whispered. He wondered if Teresa heard him.

Mr. Bueller said that if the students studied hard, at the end of the year they could go to France and be understood by the populace.

One kid raised his hand and asked, "What's 'populace'?"

"The people, the people of France."

Mr. Bueller asked if anyone knew French. Victor raised his hand, wanting to impress Teresa. The teacher beamed and said, *"Très bien. Parlez-vous français?"*

Victor didn't know what to say. The teacher wet his lips and asked something else in French.

The room grew silent. Victor felt all eyes staring at him. He tried to bluff his way out by making noises that sounded French.

"La me vava me con le grandma," he said uncertainly.

Mr. Bueller, wrinkling his face in curiosity, asked him to speak up.

Great rosebushes of red bloomed on Victor's cheeks. A river of nervous sweat ran down his palms. He felt awful. Teresa sat a few desks away, no doubt thinking he was a fool. Without looking at Mr. Bueller, Victor mumbled, "Frenchie oh wewe gee in September."

Mr. Bueller asked Victor to repeat what he had said.

"Frenchie oh wewe gee in September," Victor repeated.

Mr. Bueller understood that the boy didn't know French and turned away. He walked to the blackboard and pointed to the words on the board with his steel-edged ruler.

"*Le bateau,*" he sang.

"Le bateau," the students repeated.

"Le bateau est sur l'eau," he sang.

"Le bateau est sur l'eau."

Victor was too weak from failure to join the class. He stared at the board and wished he had taken Spanish, not French. Better yet, he wished he could start his life over. He had never been so embarrassed. He bit his thumb until he tore off a sliver of skin.

The bell sounded for fifth period, and Victor shot out of the room, avoiding the stares of the other kids, but had to return for his math book. He looked sheepishly at the teacher, who was erasing the board, then widened his eyes in terror at Teresa who stood in front of him. "I didn't

know you knew French," she said. "That was good."

Mr. Bueller looked at Victor, and Victor looked back. Oh please, don't say anything, Victor pleaded with his eyes. I'll wash your car, mow your lawn, walk your dog—anything! I'll be your best student, and I'll clean your erasers after school.

Mr. Bueller shuffled through the papers on his desk. He smiled and hummed as he sat down to work. He remembered his college years when he dated a girlfriend in borrowed cars. She thought he was rich because each time he picked her up he had a different car. It was fun until he had spent all his money on her and had to write home to his parents because he was broke.

Victor couldn't stand to look at Teresa. He was sweaty with shame. "Yeah, well, I picked up a few things from movies and books and stuff like that." They left the class together. Teresa asked him if he would help her with her French.

"Sure, anytime," Victor said.

"I won't be bothering you, will I?"

"Oh no, I like being bothered."

"*Bonjour*," Teresa said, leaving him outside her next class. She smiled and pushed wisps of hair from her face.

"Yeah, right, *bonjour*," Victor said. He turned and headed to his class. The rosebushes of shame on his face became bouquets of love. Teresa is a great girl, he thought. And Mr. Bueller is a good guy.

He raced to metal shop. After metal shop there was biology, and after biology a long sprint to the public library, where he checked out three French textbooks.

He was going to like seventh grade.

Gary Soto

ORANGES

The first time I walked
With a girl, I was twelve,
Cold, and weighted down
With two oranges in my jacket.
December. Frost cracking
Beneath my steps, my breath
Before me, then gone,
As I walked toward
Her house, the one whose
Porchlight burned yellow
Night and day, in any weather.
A dog barked at me, until
She came out pulling
At her gloves, face bright
With rouge. I smiled,
Touched her shoulder, and led
Her down the street, across
A used car lot and a line
Of newly planted trees,
Until we were breathing

Before a drugstore. We
Entered, the tiny bell
Bringing a saleslady
Down a narrow aisle of goods.
I turned to the candies
Tiered like bleachers,
And asked what she wanted—
Light in her eyes, a smile
Starting at the corners
Of her mouth. I fingered
A nickel in my pocket,
And when she lifted a chocolate
That cost a dime,
I didn't say anything.
I took the nickel from
My pocket, then an orange,
And set them quietly on
The counter. When I looked up,
The lady's eyes met mine,
And held them, knowing
Very well what it was all
About.
       Outside,
A few cars hissing past,
Fog hanging like old
Coats between the trees.
I took my girl's hand
In mine for two blocks,
Then released it to let
Her unwrap the chocolate.
I peeled my orange
That was so bright against
The gray of December
That, from some distance,
Someone might have thought
I was making a fire in my hands.

Gary Soto

THE GYMNAST

A·18

For three days of my eleventh summer I listened to my mother yap about my cousin, Issac, who was taking gymnastics. She was proud of him, she said one evening at the stove as she pounded a round steak into *carne asada* and crushed a heap of beans into *refritos*. I was jealous because I had watched my share of "Wide World of Sports" and knew that people admired an athlete who could somersault without hurting himself. I pushed aside my solitary game of Chinese checkers and spent a few minutes rolling around the backyard until I was dizzy and itchy with grass.

That Saturday, I went to Issac's house where I ate plums and sat under an aluminum arbor watching my cousin, dressed in gymnastic shorts and top, do spindly cartwheels and backflips in his backyard while he instructed, "This is the correct way." He breathed in the grassy air, leaped, and came up smiling the straightest teeth in the world.

I followed him to the front lawn. When a car passed, he did a backflip and looked out the side of his eyes to see if any of the passengers were looking. Some pointed while others looked ahead dully at the road.

My cousin was a showoff, but I figured he was allowed the limelight before one appreciative dog who had come over to look. I envied him and his cloth gymnast shoes. I liked the way they looked, slim, black and cool. They seemed special, something I could never slip onto my feet.

I ate the plums and watched him until he was sweaty and out of breath. When he was finished, I begged him to let me wear his cloth shoes. Drops of sweat fell at his feet. He looked at me with disdain, ran a yellow towel across his face, and patted his neck dry. He tore the white tape from his wrists—I liked the tape as well and tried to paste it around my wrists. He washed off his hands. I asked him about the white powder,

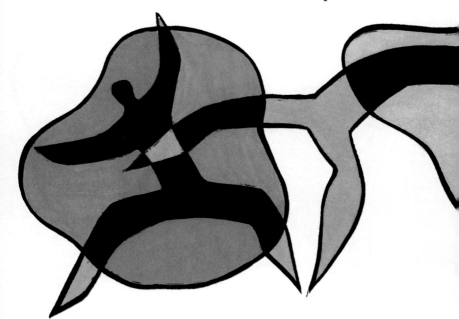

and he said it kept his hands dry. I asked him
why he needed dry hands to do cartwheels and
backflips. He said that all gymnasts kept their
hands dry, then drank from a bottle of greenish
water he said was filled with nutrients.

I asked him again if I could wear his shoes.
He slipped them off and said, "OK, just for a
while." The shoes were loose, but I liked them. I
went to the front yard with my wrists dripping
tape and my hands white as gloves. I smiled slyly
and thought I looked neat. But when I did a cart-
wheel, the shoes flew off, along with the tape,
and my cousin yelled and stomped the grass.

I was glad to get home. I was jealous and
miserable, but the next day I found a pair of old
vinyl slippers in the closet that were sort of like
gymnastic shoes. I pushed my feet into them,
tugging and wincing because they were too
small. I took a few steps, admiring my feet,
which looked like bloated water balloons, and
went outside to do cartwheels on the front lawn.

A friend skidded to a stop on his bike, one cheek fat with sunflower seeds. His mouth churned to a stop. He asked why I was wearing slippers on a hot day. I made a face at him and said that they were gymnastic shoes, not slippers. He watched me do cartwheels for a while, then rode away doing a wheelie.

I returned inside. I looked for tape to wrap my wrists, but could find only circle band-aids in the medicine cabinet. I dipped my hands in flour to keep them dry and went back outside to do cartwheels and, finally, after much hesitation, a backflip that nearly cost me my life when I landed on my head. I crawled to the shade, stars of pain pulsating in my shoulder and neck.

My brother glided by on his bike, smooth as a kite. He stared at me and asked why I was wearing slippers. I didn't answer him. My neck still hurt. He asked about the flour on my hands, and I told him to leave me alone. I turned on the hose and drank cool water.

I walked to Romain playground where I played Chinese checkers and was asked a dozen times why I was wearing slippers. I'm taking gymnastics, I lied, and these are the kind of shoes you wear. When one kid asked why I had white powder on my hands and in my hair, I gave up on Chinese checkers and returned home, my feet throbbing. But before I went inside, I took off the slippers. My toes cooled on the summery grass. I ran a garden hose on my feet and bluish ankles, and a chill ran up my back.

Dinner was a ten-minute affair of piranha-like eating and thirty minutes of washing dishes. Once finished, I returned to the backyard, where I again stuffed my feet into the slippers and did cartwheels by the dizzy dozens. After a while they were easy. I had to move on. I sucked in the summer air, along with the smoke of a far-away barbecue, and tried a backflip. I landed on my neck again, and this time I saw an orange burst behind my eyes. I lay on the grass, tired and sweaty, my feet squeezed in the vise of cruel slippers.

I watched the dusk settle and the first stars, pinpoints of unfortunate light tangled in telephone wires. I ate a plum, cussed, and pictured my cousin, who was probably cartwheeling to the audience of one sleeping dog.

Gary Soto

BLACK HAIR

At eight I was brilliant with my body.
In July, that ring of heat
We all jumped through, I sat in the bleachers
Of Romain Playground, in the lengthening
Shade that rose from our dirty feet.
The game before us was more than baseball.
It was a figure—Hector Moreno,
Quick and hard with turned muscles,
His crouch the one I assumed before an altar
Of worn baseball cards, in my room.

I came here because I was Mexican, a stick
Of light in love with those
Who could do it—the triple and hard slide,
The gloves eating balls into double plays.
What could I do with 50 pounds, my shyness,
My black torch of hair, about to go out?
Father was dead, his face no longer
Hanging over the table or our sleep,
And mother was the dream of mouths
Twisting hurt by butter knives.

In the bleachers I was brilliant with my body,
Waving players in and stomping my feet,
Growing sweaty in the presence of white shirts.
I chewed sunflower seeds. I drank water
And bit my arm through the late innings.
When Hector lined balls in deep
Center, in my mind I rounded the bases
With him, my face flared, my hair lifting
Beautifully, because we were coming home
To the arms of brown people.

Gary Soto

ON SPORTS AND YOUNG LOVE

Gary Soto

For me, sports mattered when I was a boy. In summer, I made the playground baseball team, and wore a team T-shirt that was three sizes too large, with a stretched neckline that hung like a noose around my neck. In winter, I played flag football, where a red plastic flag whipped at my thigh when I ran out for a pass. Usually the football stung my fingertips and bounced off my chest. I would blame the quarterback, the wet grass, a push from behind, the sun, the lack of sun— anyone or anything but my butterfingers.

For me, and all the kids on my block, sports was why you ate Wheaties and stared at the cereal box of athletes going up for a lay-up or reaching skyward for a finger-tip catch in the end zone. Sports was why I improvised coffee-can weights in the backyard and went around with

my shirt off, chest puffed out like a chicken. Sports was why I returned home holding my nose: on the baseball diamond, a grounder took an awkward leap and slapped me in the face.

I loved sports. And what I liked best about them was wearing a uniform. That's why I was jealous of my cousin, Issac, who, at twelve and a year older than me, was enrolled in a gymnastics class. I was jealous because he wore a tidy little gymnast uniform and dainty slippers. *I* wanted to wear a uniform and slippers. Wearing a uniform, even a gymnastic outfit with slippers, would separate me from the crowd. That's why when my older brother Rick made junior varsity football and came home with his shoulder pads I strapped them on when he wasn't looking. Even on my bony shoulders, they made me look like I could conquer the world.

By seventh grade girls were no longer my

enemy. They had started wearing make-up and looking cute with their little purses. They even started liking us, the boys, who only a year earlier were dirty from playing sports. Of course, I started noticing them as well. I started to comb my hair and brush my teeth two times before I took off for school. I became curious. I tried to be around them, especially at break when one day I noticed that they chewed their gum with their mouths closed. I noticed my jaw jumping around and figured out that I chewed with my mouth wide open. I saw then the difference between boys and girls.

My story "Seventh Grade" is about liking girls. It is about Victor trying to impress Teresa; he is pretending that he can speak French, the most romantic language in the world, or so we are told. The story, then, is about learning to speak to a girl. Victor mumbles nonsense and we like him for that. Sure, he is embarrassing himself, but he's the first one out there, chattering "Frenchie oh wewe gee in September." We applaud him for his nerve.

The story is also about getting yourself in trouble. Wanting to impress Teresa, Victor finds himself trapped by his lie—opening his mouth to say he could speak French. How many times have we gotten ourselves in trouble when we have said we could do something when we knew we couldn't?

Some of you may ask, Did this really happen? Yes, it did. But it happened in my wife's high-school Spanish class. She never figured out what the boy was saying, and the teacher could only press his hands to his ears. The boy was ruining the language spoken by Don Quixote, himself a dreamer who chased windmills near the border of France.

THINKING ABOUT IT

1. If you asked Gary Soto what his characters' *goals* are, what do you think he would say? If he asked *you* what your goals are, what would *you* say? Sometimes authors offer advice through their characters. Does that happen here? Explain.

2. What is the evidence that Gary Soto knows and likes seventh-graders—or do you think that he doesn't understand what it's like to be in the seventh grade?

3. The time is twenty years from now. You have a job that calls for you to write, sing, draw, photograph, dance, or speak about "Seventh-Graders of Twenty Years Ago." Think of seven things you consider most important or most typical about today's seventh-graders.

Another Book by Gary Soto

A fire in my hands is a collection of poems about young people, followed by a few of Soto's ideas on poetry.

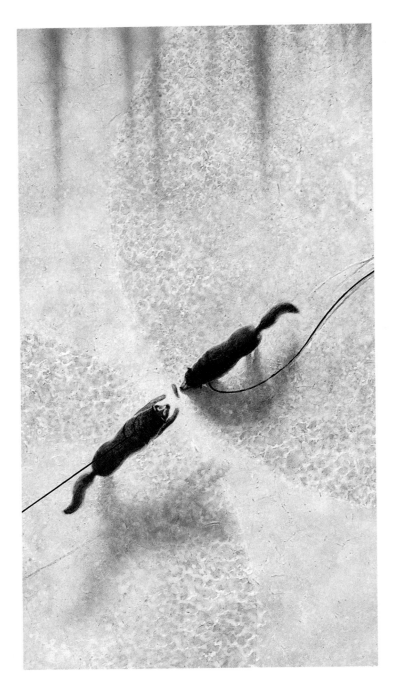

And The Dogs Could Teach Me

from *Woodsong*

C old can be very strange. Not the cold felt running from the house to the bus or the car to the store; not the chill in the air on a fall morning, but deep cold.

Serious cold.

Forty, fifty, even sixty below zero—actual temperature, not windchill—seems to change everything. Steel becomes brittle and breaks, shatters; breath taken straight into the throat will freeze the lining and burst blood vessels; eyes exposed too long will freeze; fingers and toes freeze, turn black, and break off. These are all known, normal parts of intense cold.

But it changes beauty as well. Things are steeped in a new clarity, a clear focus. Sound seems to ring and the very air seems to be filled with diamonds when ice crystals form.

On a river in Alaska while training I once saw a place where a whirlpool had frozen into a cone, open at the bottom like a beautiful trap waiting to suck the whole team down. When I stopped to look at it, with the water roaring through at the bottom, the dogs became nervous and stared down into the center as if mystified and were very glad when we moved on.

After a time I stopped trapping. That change—as with many changes—occurred because of the dogs. As mentioned, I had hunted when I was young, trapping and killing many animals. I never thought it wrong until the dogs came. And then it was a simple thing, almost a silly thing, that caused the change.

Columbia had a sense of humor and I saw it.

In the summer the dogs live in the kennel area, each dog with his own house, on a chain that allows him to move in a circle. They can only run with the wheeled carts on cool nights, and sometimes they get bored being tied up. To alleviate the boredom we give the dogs large beef bones to chew and play with. They get a new bone every other day or so. These bones are the center of much contention—we call them Bone Wars. Sometimes dogs clear across the kennel will hold their bones up in the air, look at each other, raise their hair, and start growling at each other, posturing and bragging about their bones.

But not Columbia.

Usually Columbia just chewed on his bone until the meat was gone. Then he buried it and waited for the next bone. I never saw him fight or get involved in Bone Wars and I always thought him a simple—perhaps a better word would be primitive—dog, basic and very wolf-like, until one day when I was sitting in the kennel.

I had a notebook and I was sitting on the side of Cookie's roof, writing — the dogs are good company for working — when I happened to notice Columbia doing something strange.

He was sitting quietly on the outside edge of his circle, at the maximum length of his chain. With one paw he was pushing his bone — which still had a small bit of meat on it — out and away from him, toward the next circle.

Next to Columbia was a dog named Olaf. While Columbia was relatively passive, Olaf was very aggressive. Olaf always wanted to fight and he spent much time arguing over bones, females, the weather — anything and everything that caught his fancy. He was much scarred from fighting, with notched ears and lines on his muzzle, but he was a very good dog — strong and honest — and we liked him.

Being next to Columbia, Olaf had tried many times to get him to argue or bluster but Columbia always ignored him.

Until this morning.

Carefully, slowly, Columbia pushed the bone toward Olaf's circle.

And of all the things that Olaf was—tough, strong, honest—he wasn't smart. As they say, some are smarter than others, and some are still not so smart, and then there was Olaf. It wouldn't be fair to call Olaf dumb—dogs don't measure those things like people—but even in the dog world he would not be known as a whip. Kind of a big bully who was also a bit of a doofus.

When he saw Columbia pushing the bone toward him, he began to reach for it. Straining against his chain, turning and trying to get far-ther and farther, he reached as far as he could with the middle toe on his right front foot, the claw going out as far as possible.

But not quite far enough. Columbia had measured it to the millimeter. He slowly pushed the bone until it was so close that Olaf's claw— with Olaf straining so hard his eyes bulged—just barely touched it.

Columbia sat back and watched Olaf strain-ing and pushing and fighting and when this had gone on for a long time—many minutes—and Olaf was still straining for all he was worth, Columbia leaned back and laughed.

"Heh, heh, heh . . ."

Then Columbia walked away.

And I could not kill or trap any longer.

It happened almost that fast. I had seen dogs with compassion for each other and their young, and with anger and joy and hate and love but this humor went into me more than the other things.

It was so complicated.

To make the joke up in his mind, the joke with the bone and the bully, and then set out to do it, carefully and quietly, to do it, then laugh and walk away—all of it was so complicated, so complex, that it triggered a chain reaction in my mind.

If Columbia could do that, I thought, if a dog could do that, then a wolf could do that. If a wolf could do that, then a deer could do that. If a deer could do that, then a beaver, and a squirrel, and a bird, and, and, and . . .

And I quit trapping then. It was wrong for me to kill. But I had this problem. I had gone over some kind of line with the dogs, gone back into some primitive state of exaltation that I wanted to study. I wanted to run them and learn from them. But it seemed to be wasteful (the word *immature* also comes to mind) to just run them. I thought I had to have a trapline to justify running the dogs, so I kept the line.

But I did not trap. I ran the country, and camped and learned from the dogs and studied where I would have trapped if I were going to trap. I took many imaginary beaver and muskrat but I did no more sets and killed no more animals. I will not kill anymore.

Yet the line existed. Somehow in my mind—and until writing this I have never told another person about this—the line still existed and when I had "trapped" in one area I would extend the line to "trap" in another, as is proper when you actually trap. Somehow the phony trapping gave me a purpose for running the dogs, and would until I began to train them for the Iditarod, a dog-sled race across Alaska, which I had read about in *Alaska* magazine.

But it was on one of these "trapping" runs that I got my third lesson, or awakening.

There was a point where an old logging trail went through a small, sharp-sided gully—a tiny canyon. The trail came down one wall of the gully—a drop of fifty or so feet—then scooted across a frozen stream and up the other side. It might have been a game trail that was slightly widened, or an old foot trail that had not caved in. Whatever it was, I came onto it in the middle of January. The dogs were very excited. New trails always get them tuned up and they were fairly smoking as we came to the edge of the gully.

I did not know it was there and had been letting them run, not riding the sled brake to slow them, and we virtually shot off the edge.

The dogs stayed on the trail but I immediately lost all control and went flying out into space with the sled. As I did, I kicked sideways and caught my knee on a sharp snag, felt the wood enter under the kneecap and tear it loose.

I may have screamed then.

The dogs ran out on the ice of the stream but I fell onto it. As these things often seem to happen, the disaster snowballed.

The trail crossed the stream directly at the top of a small, frozen waterfall with about a twenty-foot drop. Later I saw the beauty of it, the falling lobes of blue ice that had grown as the water froze and refroze, layering on itself. . . .

But at the time I saw nothing. I hit the ice of the stream bed like dropped meat, bounced once, then slithered over the edge of the waterfall

and dropped another twenty feet onto the frozen pond below, landing on the torn and separated kneecap.

I have been injured several times running dogs—cracked ribs, a broken left leg, a broken left wrist, various parts frozen or cut or bitten while trying to stop fights—but nothing ever felt like landing on that knee.

I don't think I passed out so much as my brain simply exploded.

Again, I'm relatively certain I must have screamed or grunted, and then I wasn't aware of much for two, perhaps three minutes as I squirmed around trying to regain some part of my mind.

When things settled down to something I could control, I opened my eyes and saw that my snow pants and the jeans beneath were ripped in a jagged line for about a foot. Blood was welling out of the tear, soaking the cloth and the ice underneath the wound.

Shock and pain came in waves and I had to close my eyes several times. All of this was in minutes that seemed like hours and I realized that I was in serious trouble. Contrary to popular belief, dog teams generally do not stop and wait for a musher who falls off. They keep going, often for many miles.

Lying there on the ice I knew I could not walk. I didn't think I could stand without some kind of crutch, but I knew I couldn't walk. I was a good twenty miles from home, at least eight or nine miles from any kind of farm or dwelling.

It may as well have been ten thousand miles.

There was some self-pity creeping in, and

not a little chagrin at being stupid enough to just let them run when I didn't know the country. I was trying to skootch myself up to the bank of the gully to get into a more comfortable position when I heard a sound over my head.

I looked up and there was Obeah looking over the top of the waterfall, down at me.

I couldn't at first believe it.

He whined a couple of times, moved back and forth as if he might be going to drag the team over the edge, then disappeared from view. I heard some more whining and growling, then a scrabbling sound, and was amazed to see that he had taken the team back up the side of the gully and dragged them past the waterfall to get on the gully wall just over me.

They were in a horrible tangle but he dragged them along the top until he was well below the waterfall, where he scrambled down the bank with the team almost literally falling on

him. They dragged the sled up the frozen stream bed to where I was lying.

On the scramble down the bank Obeah had taken them through a thick stand of cockleburs. Great clumps of burrs wadded between their ears and down their backs.

He pulled them up to me, concern in his eyes and making a soft whine, and I reached into his ruff and pulled his head down and hugged him and was never so happy to see anybody probably in my life. Then I felt something and looked down to see one of the other dogs—named Duberry—licking the wound in my leg.

She was not licking with the excitement that prey blood would cause, but with the gentle licking that she would use when cleaning a pup, a wound lick.

I brushed her head away, fearing infection, but she persisted. After a moment I lay back and let her clean it, still holding onto Obeah's ruff, holding onto a friend.

And later I dragged myself around and untangled them and unloaded part of the sled and crawled in and tied my leg down. We made it home that way, with me sitting in the sled: and later when my leg was sewed up and healing and I was sitting in my cabin with the leg propped up on pillows by the wood stove; later when all the pain was gone and I had all the time I needed to think of it . . . later I thought of the dogs.

How they came back to help me, perhaps to save me. I knew that somewhere in the dogs, in their humor and the way they thought, they had great, old knowledge; they had something we had lost.

And the dogs could teach me.

Thinking About It

1. Almost everyone has a true story about the unusualness of some animal or other. Surely you have one too. How would you tell it to Gary Paulsen?

2. Authors give evidence for their decisions. Gary Paulsen decided to give up trapping. What evidence in the selection shows that he means it?

3. If dogs could speak—! What would Columbia and Olaf be saying to themselves and to each other during the "Bone Wars" incident?

Another Book About Animals

James Herriot's Dog Stories by James Herriot includes fifty stories about dogs and their reactions to the vets who treat them.

Opera, Karate, And Bandits

from *The Land I Lost*

When she was eighty years old my grandmother was still quite strong. She could use her own teeth to eat corn on the cob or to chew on sugar plants to extract juice from them. Every two days she walked for more than an hour to reach the marketplace, carrying a heavy load of food with her, and then spent another hour walking back home. And even though she was quite old, traces of her beauty still lingered on: Her hands, her feet, her face revealed that she had been an attractive young woman. Nor did time do much damage to the youthful spirit of my grandmother.

One of her great passions was theater, and this passion never diminished with age. No matter how busy she was, she never missed a show when there was a group of actors in town. If no actors visited our hamlet for several months, she would organize her own show in which she was the manager, the producer, and the young leading lady, all at the same time.

My grandmother's own plays were always melodramas inspired by books she had read and by what she had seen on the stage. She always chose her favorite grandson to play the role of the hero, who would, without fail, marry the heroine at the end and live happily ever after. And when my sisters would tell her that she was getting too old to play the role of the young heroine anymore, my grandmother merely replied: "Anybody can play this role if she's young at heart."

When I was a little boy my grandmother often took me to see the opera. She knew Chinese mythology by heart, and the opera was often a dramatization of this mythology. On one special occasion, during the Lunar New Year celebrations—my favorite holiday, because children could do anything they wanted and by tradition no one could scold them—I accompanied my grandmother to the opera.

When we reached the theater I wanted to go in immediately. But my grandmother wanted to linger at the entrance and talk to her friends. She chatted for more than an hour. Finally we entered the theater, and at that moment the "Faithful One" was onstage, singing sadly. The "Faithful One" is a common character in Chinese opera. He could be a good minister, or a valiant general, or someone who loved and served his king faithfully. But in the end he is unjustly persecuted by the king, whose opinion of him has been changed by the lies of the "Flatterer," another standard character.

When my grandmother saw the "Faithful One" onstage she looked upset and gave a great sigh. I was too interested in what was happening to ask her the reason, and we spent the next five hours watching the rest of the opera. Sometimes I cried because my grandmother cried at the pitiful situation of the "Faithful One." Sometimes I became as angry as my grandmother did at the wickedness of the "Flatterer."

When we went home that night my grandmother was quite sad. She told my mother that she would have bad luck in the following year because when we entered the theater, the "Faithful One" was onstage. I was puzzled. I told my grandmother that she was confused. It would be a good year for us because we saw the good guy first. But my mother said, "No, son. The 'Faithful One' always is in trouble and it takes him many years to vindicate himself. Our next year is going to be like one of his bad years."

So, according to my mother's and grandmother's logic, we would have been much better off in the new year if we had been lucky enough to see the villain first!

M y grandmother had married a man whom she loved with all her heart, but who was totally different from her. My grandfather was very shy, never laughed loudly, and always spoke very softly. And physically he was not as strong as my grandmother. But he excused his lack of physical strength by saying that he was a "scholar."

About three months after their marriage, my grandparents were in a restaurant and a rascal began to insult my grandfather because he looked

weak and had a pretty wife. At first he just made insulting remarks, such as, "Hey! Wet chicken! This is no place for a weakling!"

My grandfather wanted to leave the restaurant even though he and my grandmother had not yet finished their meal. But my grandmother pulled his shirt sleeve and signaled him to remain seated. She continued to eat and looked as if nothing had happened.

Tired of yelling insults without any result, the rascal got up from his table, moved over to my grandparents' table, and grabbed my grandfather's chopsticks. My grandmother immediately wrested the chopsticks from him and struck the rascal on his cheekbone with her elbow. The blow was so quick and powerful that he lost his balance and fell on the floor. Instead of finishing him off, as any street fighter would do, my grandmother let the rascal recover from the blow. But as soon as he got up again, he kicked over the table between him and my grandmother, making food and drink fly all over the place. Before he could do anything else, my grandmother kicked him on the chin. The kick was so swift that my grandfather didn't even see it. He only heard a heavy thud, and then saw the rascal tumble backward and collapse on the ground.

All the onlookers were surprised and delighted, especially the owner of the restaurant. Apparently the rascal, one of the best karate fighters of our area, came to his restaurant every day and left without paying for his food or drink, but the owner was too afraid to confront him.

While the rascal's friends tried to revive him, everyone else surrounded my grandmother and asked her who had taught her karate. She said, "Who else? My husband!"

After the fight at the restaurant people assumed that my grandfather knew karate very well but refused to use it for fear of killing someone. In reality, my grandmother had received special training in karate from my great-great uncle from the time she was eight years old.

Anyway, after that incident, my grandfather never had to worry again. Anytime he had some business downtown, people treated him very well. And whenever anyone happened to bump into him on the street, they bowed to my grandfather in a very respectful way.

When my father was about ten years old a group of bandits attacked our house. There had been a very poor harvest that year, and bandits had already attacked several homes in other hamlets. My grandmother had a premonition this would also happen to them, so she devised a plan. In case of danger, she would carry the children to safety, and my grandfather would carry the bow and arrows, a bottle of poison, and the box containing the family jewels.

It was night when the bandits came. My grandfather became scared to death and forgot his part of the plan, but my grandmother re-

mained very calm. She
led her husband and
children to safety
through a secret back
door that opened into
a double hedge of
cactus that allowed a
person to walk inside,
undetected, to the
banana grove. When
they were safely inside
the banana grove, my
grandfather realized
that he had forgotten
the bow and arrows
and the bottle of poi-

son. So my grandmother stole back into the
house and retrieved the weapons.

The bandits were still trying to smash
through our very solid front door when she
sneaked out of the house for the second time.
She dipped one arrow in poison and crawled
around to the front of the house near the bandits.
But, upon second thought, she put the poisoned
arrow aside and took another arrow and carefully
aimed at the leg of the bandit leader. When the
arrow hit his thigh the bandit let out a loud cry
and fell backward.

The night was so dark that none of the bandits knew where the arrow had come from. And
moments later, friends started arriving and began
to attack them from the road in front of our
house. The bandits panicked and left in a hurry.
But my grandmother spent the rest of the night
with her family in the banana grove, just in case
the bandits came back.

W hen my grandmother became older she felt sick once in a while. Before the arrival of the doctor, she would order everybody in the house to look sad. And during the consultation with the doctor she acted as if she were much sicker than she really was. My grandmother felt that she had to make herself look really sick so that the doctor would give her good medicine. She told the doctor that she had a pain in the head, in the shoulders, in the chest, in the back, in the limbs—pain everywhere. Finally the doctor would become confused and wouldn't know what could be wrong with her.

Whenever the doctor left, my mother would sneak out of the house, meet him at the other side of the garden, and tell him exactly where my grandmother hurt.

Two or three days later my grandmother usually felt much better. But before the doctor arrived for another visit she ordered us to look sad again—not as sad as the first time, but quite sad. She would tell the doctor that her situation had improved a little bit but that she still felt quite sick. My grandmother thought that if she told the doctor she had been feeling much better he would stop giving her good medicine. When the doctor left my mother sneaked out of the house again and informed him of the real condition of my grandmother.

I don't think my grandmother ever guessed it was my mother's reports to the doctor, and not her acting, that helped her get well.

One morning my grandmother wanted me to go outside with her. We climbed a little hill that looked over the whole area, and when we got to the top she looked at the rice field below, the mountain on the horizon, and especially at the river. As a young girl she had often brought her herd of water buffaloes to the river to drink while she swam with the other children of the village. Then we visited the graveyard where her husband and some of her children were buried. She touched her husband's tombstone and said, "Dear, I will join you soon." And then we walked back to the garden and she gazed at the fruit trees her husband had planted, a new one for each time she had given birth to a child. Finally, before we left the garden my sister joined us, and the two of them fed a few ducks swimming in the pond.

That evening my grandmother did not eat much of her dinner. After dinner she combed her hair and put on her best dress. We thought that she was going to go out again, but instead she went to her bedroom and told us that she didn't want to be disturbed.

The family dog seemed to sense something was amiss, for he kept looking anxiously at everybody and whined from time to time. At midnight my mother went to my grandmother's room and found that she had died, with her eyes shut, as if she were sleeping normally.

It took me a long time to get used to the reality that my grandmother had passed away. Wherever I was, in the house, in the garden, out on the fields, her face always appeared so clearly to me. And even now, many years later, I still have the feeling that my last conversation with her has happened only a few days before.

Thinking About It

1. If you were writing your autobiography, and if you decided to put in a chapter about bandits, and if you wrote that bandits had attacked your home. . . . Well, what would you say?

2. When it comes to marriage, do likes attract or do opposites attract? Are the grandmother and grand-father in this selection alike or opposite? Give examples from the selection to explain your answer.

3. You are designing a modern retirement home for active, elderly people like the narrator's grand-mother. You have to convince the owner of the home that these people need more than a rocking chair and a TV. What would you say?

M V P

The highlight of my two years in junior high school was getting the key to my own locker. This was the big time—it announced the approach of adolescence; I was deemed old enough for possessions that needed to be locked up.

The same day we received our locker keys we got a long set of rules and a privilege card. We weren't allowed to go anywhere without the yellow card; teachers signed us in and out of class and we were punished if we were caught in the halls without permission. The principal took our cards away if we broke too many rules, which meant that we had no chance to use the bathrooms or drinking fountains except in the two minutes between classes.

On one hand, they admitted that we were growing up; but on the other hand, they regulated everything we did. It was a frustrating time for all concerned. The teachers weren't thrilled to be disciplining us all the time instead of teaching, and we chafed under the routine.

There were similar problems at home. I thought my parents were too strict and old-fashioned. They were still telling me when to go to bed, what to wear, and how long to talk on the phone. I wanted them to see that I was becoming a young woman and could make some decisions for myself. When I defied them they were more determined than ever to uphold their rules.

We had some good moments when I just decided to be honest with them. One day some older kids made fun of my white ankle socks on the bus; I was still wearing my oxford shoes in the seventh grade. They pointed at me and called me names while I tried not to cry. When I got home I told my mother I wouldn't be wearing white socks anymore. She agreed that I was probably too old for them and that was that. On another occasion I asked for permission to begin shaving my legs; Mom showed me how. I was grateful to her, but at times like those I wished I had an older sister to go to for advice and comfort. My brothers were great, but I couldn't ask them to teach me womanly things. Once in a while Mom had to step away from her post as an authority figure and act like a sister, difficult as it was for both of us. I was embarrassed about putting her in that role, even to teach me to shave my legs, so I usually turned to friends for help. But I always envied my friends who had sisters.

I learned to live within my parents' boundaries because they were willing to listen to reason. They almost never changed their minds, but they were open to calm appeals and they could surprise me with leniency at the oddest times. School was different—nobody cared what I thought of the rules there.

As an adult I can understand my junior high school teachers, but it was hard to be their student. The building was overcrowded—we were still waiting for the new high school to open—and dark, old, and depressing. We didn't have any extracurricular activities to enjoy after school, so we all came and went at the same hours. We did everything together, day after day, like a herd of antelopes moving on the veld. We were a jumpy, bored mob—it was no wonder that they needed so many rules to keep us in line.

Going into the high school was like leaving a minimum security prison for the outside world. Suddenly we had choices to make; nobody was telling us where to be and what to do all the time. The Cape Elizabeth schools were led by Superintendent Harold Raynolds, Jr., who felt that we should be given more control of our time in school. The high school offered a series of nine- and eighteen-week mini-courses in English and Social Studies from which we could pick and choose, while the other departments held on to their traditional curricula. In free periods we could elect to swim, study in the library, sit out on a sunny hillside, eat, or do anything else that didn't involve leaving campus, disturbing classes, or breaking rules.

People told Mr. Raynolds he was wrong. They said high-school kids would tear the building apart unless they were kept under the strictest discipline. Here the town had spent a fortune to build a new school and he was going to let it be destroyed.

But they underestimated us. We were grateful for the building and for the freedom to

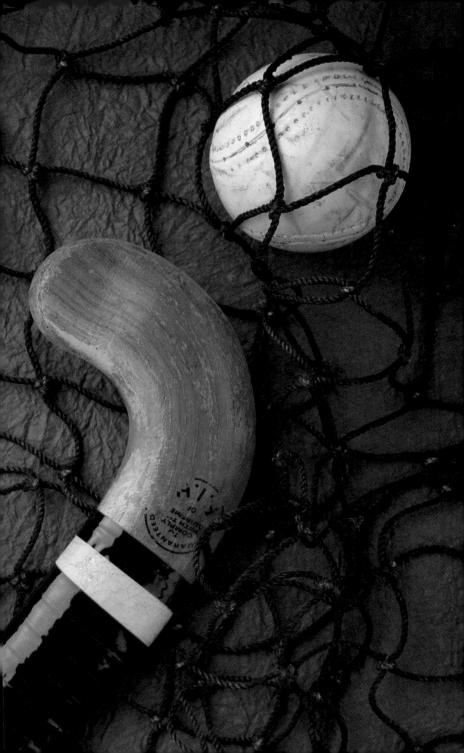

experiment with it. We understood that Mr. Raynolds was depending on us to behave like responsible people. In the four years I spent at that school, I heard of only one act of vandalism: somebody set fire to a wastebasket in the boys' bathroom.

It was difficult to search out the basics in the humanities curriculum and I had to scramble to make up for holes in that foundation when I got to college. Perhaps we needed a bit more structure and less choice. But I recently heard a former teacher refer to those days as "the time of select-an-education: one from column A, one from column B." It wasn't like that. It was the early 1970s and freedom was called for. The Raynolds system worked for me, as it did for most of the kids I knew. After two years of junior high, slumbering in the knowledge that someone else was making every decision, this was a welcome awakening.

The choices weren't confined to academic pursuits. At last I had a chance to participate in after-school activities. I told Mom I was trying out for field hockey. She was thrilled: field hockey had been her favorite sport in high school. I was worried because I'd never played before, but Mom assured me I could pick up the basics in a hurry.

Tryouts began the first week of school. The coaches, Paula Smith and Andrea Cayer, put us through hard workouts for several days; I made the junior varsity squad and occasionally played varsity. I played the center and right inner forward positions: my job was to get the ball and tear down the field with it toward the opposite team's goal.

Field hockey was the only sport open to girls in the fall; it was no easy thing to gain a spot on the team. For me it was like belonging to a popular club, and it made the transition to high school much easier. There is a camaraderie in sports, even among athletes who compete against one another, that I haven't encountered anywhere else.

Sometimes I like to be around other marathoners just because they are the only people who really understand what I do. People call me a natural athlete—and in some respects I suppose I am—but to say that is to dismiss a world of effort. Other runners know how hard I've had to train; their respect is always the sweetest to earn. Field hockey gave me my first bout with the "natural athlete" label.

I wasn't a natural hockey player. I had the speed and toughness needed, but I wasn't coordinated enough to handle the stick exceptionally well. In playing the forward positions, it is important to make good passes and score when the occasion arises. I practiced extra hours, laboring to learn stickwork. To keep my place on the team in the meantime, I showed the coaches I could run and use my head. They gave me the leeway I needed, and eventually I improved my ball-handling talents to the point where I could be counted on for a goal almost every game. It took the same kind of patience running takes.

The trick was never to get complacent. I liked praise as much as anyone else, and I was praised a great deal on the hockey field. But I knew I was capable of more—that kept me honest. I would squirm under compliments most of the time, not in false modesty, but because I had a voice inside that said, "Watch it." The voice kept me ever aware of the fact that I wasn't reaching my potential. Just because people thought I was a good hockey player didn't mean I *was;* only I knew whether I was giving a hundred percent. When I played as hard and as well as my body told me I could, I would be pleased.

Athletes understand things like that. I've been asked why I didn't quit running marathons after the Olympics, and it's hard to explain. But to an athlete, I can say, "Look, I haven't given it everything I've got yet," and the other head nods. Understood. The girls on the hockey team were equally tuned in: they let me be unhappy about a so-so performance without reminding me that some people would be delighted with it. They knew I was my own best motivator.

I did latch on to other sources of inspiration, though. Oddly enough, the coaches of the opposing teams often spurred me. Field hockey was taken very seriously in our league, so a number of good coaches were involved. The better they were, the more I tried to play well when we met their teams. I always wanted to do my best around the people who loved hockey. It was my way of demonstrating respect for their accomplishments as coaches and former players.

Because of this penchant, I may have played my best hockey at the Merestead Hockey and Lacrosse Camp during the summers of 1972 and 1974. Some of the staff members had been on British and United States national teams, some were college coaches, and all had long backgrounds in the sport. We played all day every day for a week. I was usually exhausted in the late afternoon, but since we had a free hour between our last practice and dinner I tried to run a couple of miles a day. By the summer of 1974 I was in a running routine that was hard to break, but I was so active on the field that my evening outing was usually a faint trot. Still, I enjoyed pushing myself to do it.

Most of our evenings were devoted to hockey. As long as we could see, we played, and our instructors mixed in with us. There were no drills and very few whistles then; we were allowed to play vigorously. I knew I was getting the best competition I was ever likely to have, so I tried especially hard.

I loved playing for Andrea Cayer. She was different from any coach I'd had before and I treated her differently. I didn't have a burning desire to show her what I could do, for one thing. Her whole attitude said she thought we were terrific kids who could do whatever we set our minds to. She was no more skeptical of my talent than she was of the ground under her feet: she supposed the talent was there and wasn't planning to change her mind unless I proved her wrong. Her confidence gave me confidence. I like keeping track of myself, by myself. Andrea knew how to admonish or encourage me when it was appropriate, but she showed me that I was growing up and didn't need the supervision of Coach Legree. I've never wanted much coaching since then.

The team itself was an inspiration; everyone worked. While the local sports writers hadn't yet begun to give any girls' sport except swimming much attention, they did a decent job with hockey—we could always find some mention of our games after the golf scores from Florida.

I liked belonging to the team as much as I'd known I would back in the dark days of junior high. The satisfaction of striding around school wearing the team jacket, of having teachers I respected comment on well-played games, and of being part of a friendly, supportive group was immense. The actual playing was what I liked best, but the attendant friendships and the glory of being on a winning team didn't hurt.

Nor did the fact that I received the Most Valuable Player award after my junior season. The MVP was usually a senior, so even while I was luxuriating in success I was feeling guilty about robbing someone who wouldn't get another chance at the award. Worse, I was the track MVP freshman year. While I stood at the podium and listened to Paula Smith, the track coach, say nice things about me, I wished I could share the awards with my teammates. Their efforts helped me shine, especially in a team sport like field hockey. I wanted to say that I would have been mauled on the field without them, that we'd all worked hard for the same goals, and that nobody deserved to take so much credit. But in those days I didn't have the words. Besides, there were few speeches at the athletic association banquet. You heard your name, your face turned red, and you walked up to accept the trophy.

Maybe I deserved to be MVP in track, if you accept the idea that running is a solitary sport in which the glory belongs to the individual. I didn't think so at age fifteen and I don't now. I knew I wouldn't be as good as I was without competition from my teammates. I might have worked harder than the others because running was so agreeable to me, but they were the standards by which I measured myself. Even today I can't take full credit for a good race. I have to leave my home in Freeport a couple of times a month to find running competition; I drive to Boston and run on the track with athletes who will give me a workout. If it wasn't for their pushing I wouldn't be the same runner. I do most of my training alone, but I can't practice in a vacuum; and I certainly can't compete in one.

I'm grateful to have made this discovery so early in my career. When the high-school team went to a meet, I wanted to do well for the team, not for myself.

Granted, stardom for a woman in track wasn't really imaginable in those days. If I had been thinking ahead to a lucrative career in sports I would have stuck to tennis. Chris Evert, Billie Jean King, and others were getting some deserved respect for women's tennis. But nobody was making a living by running.

Of course I was aware of my athletic talent, but it seemed to me that if I allowed myself to think I was as good as people said, I would have a long way to fall. That's why the prizes, honors, and attention don't affect me now. I'm always pleased and touched—who could help being thrilled about the Sullivan and Jesse Owens awards?—but I can't let myself believe I deserve such things. I'll lose my edge if I do that. If I start running for the awards, my career is over. I'm still running because I have a goal to reach, a time that has eluded me up to now.

In high school as now, I was motivated by success. My freshman year was so successful I couldn't believe it. The winning ways of the field hockey team sustained me even after the season was over, which was a good thing—I had less joyful experiences with the basketball team. I tried out for basketball because so many of my friends were on the team, and because it would fill a void during the weekdays when I wasn't skiing. I played on the junior varsity squad for the next three winters and never gained the coach's confidence. As soon as things got tight, I came out of the game. In my senior year I auditioned for the school play instead and loved doing it.

Throughout the winter of my freshman year I looked forward to track season, all the more so because Peter had given me a pair of running shoes for Christmas. I had wanted them for a long time, but Mom and Dad never gave me any running-related gear because they didn't want to push me into sports. These weren't my first speciality shoes—I'd bought a pair for tennis the summer before—but they were special. For years I had watched Andy and Peter compete on their high school team in Chuck Taylor shoes by Converse; people would laugh at them today. They had curled toes and looked professional. When I was twelve I took my best pair of sneakers and put them in a vise, trying to bend the toes. I had to wait two years for a pair of bona fide running shoes, but they were worth it.

They worked as advertised, too. I ran well enough to attract attention from the newspapers that spring. I tried to do everything, from running the 100, 200, and relay to the long jump. The good races are a blur in my memory, though: what I remember best is a bad experience with a coach.

I dove for the finish line while running the 100-yard dash in a meet against a western Maine school. I was brushing the dirt off my knees when the other team's coach walked over and said, "Cape may be famous for its swim team, but you don't dive on the track." She made it sound as if I had done something terribly wrong, almost illegal. I'd beaten the best sprinter in the Triple C conference, so the coach came after me out of frustration; I didn't know that at the time. She made me feel awful.

Incidents like that taught me not to crumble under adversity. If that coach meant to make me cry, she succeeded; but if she meant to break my concentration, she failed. I was all the more intent on winning after her comment—I wanted to show her I could win without diving. When her sprinter and I squared off in the 200, I won standing straight.

I can take a bad situation and make it work to my advantage: that's part of what mental toughness means. I don't know where it comes from, but it's the one attribute I know I can count on to get me through the bad times. Maybe it's a cumulative thing: the more adversity you have to face, the tougher you get (provided you meet and beat it). My body may fail me, but my head never has. There's a switch I can throw that puts me into high concentration: I focus one hundred percent on the immediate goal; I forget I have a body; I don't feel pain. It's a gift that took some nurturing. I had to use people like that coach for my own purposes. The day I refused to let her neutralize me, I took a step toward recovering from knee surgery in time to win an Olympic gold medal.

Thinking About It

1. "Something like that happened to me too. No, it wasn't a locker key but it was something that suddenly made me feel, you know, *really* grown up." Use your own experience to finish this reader's statement.

2. Joan Benoit says she has mental toughness. What does she mean by that? What in this selection would you use to prove that she does or does not have this toughness? And, by the way, do *you* have it? Why or why not?

3. "You deserve a medal!" Who does? Name someone you know who deserves a medal. For what? What sort of medal? A medal with *what* written on it? Why?

ELLEN CONFORD

I'll Take Spaghetti

"Pizza," I moaned. "French fries. Chocolate graham crackers. Big Macs. Thick shakes. Eclairs. Spaghetti and meatballs."

"Carrot sticks," said Judy. "Celery. Green pepper strips. An eight-ounce cup of bouillon."

"You don't offer a drowning man a glass of water!" I cried. "I can't stand it anymore. I've got paper cuts all over my fingers from opening those bouillon packets. If I eat one more carrot stick I'm going to turn yellow. That can happen, you know. Too much Vitamin A makes you turn yellow. *Listen to me.* I've got to have something that doesn't crunch when I eat it or I'm going to die."

"Bouillon doesn't crunch," Judy pointed out. "And you're not going to die. You've got to stop thinking about food all the time. You've got to put food in its proper place. It's just not that important."

"When you've got enough, it's not important. When you're starving—"

"You're not starving. You're on a perfectly adequate diet of twelve hundred calories a day, and no one starves on that."

"I do!"

It was true. I'd only been on the diet three days, but I was ready to throw in the sponge. (Sponge cake. Devil's food cake. *Pizza*.) The doctor had given me that "perfectly adequate diet" and told me I could expect to lose two pounds a week. Since I had to lose twenty pounds, that meant ten weeks of carrot sticks, bouillon, and broiled chicken.

"I'll never make it."

"Of course you'll make it," Judy said. "I have faith in you."

"I don't know why. I never made it any of the other times."

This wasn't the first diet I'd been on. I'd been overweight ever since sixth grade, and every attempt at losing my excess poundage had been a dismal failure.

I'd tried the grapefruit diet, the kelp diet, the Miracle Alfalfa diet, the Beverly Hills Diet, the Scarsdale diet, the Oshkosh diet—if it was written up in a magazine, or had "miracle" in its name, I'd tried it.

Nothing worked. By the second day I'd get

discouraged. By the third day I'd be depressed. By the fourth day, visions of Mallomars danced in my head.

So I always ended up saying, "What's the use? I'll never lose all that weight." Looking at myself in the mirror and knowing I'd never look the way I wanted to depressed me so much that the only way I could cheer myself up was to eat an entire box of chocolate chip cookies.

After which I got depressed all over again because I hated myself for eating an entire box of chocolate chip cookies. And what was the point of going back on my diet when I'd already ruined it by eating all those cookies?

"This is different," Judy said. "Everybody knows crash diets don't work. Those others were all faddy things. This is the first time you've tried a normal, sensible diet. I mean, look at all the things you're allowed to eat."

"Are you kidding?"

The doctor had given me this mimeographed list with two columns of food on it. The first column was headed "Foods to Avoid." The second column was "Permissible Foods." The first column had about a hundred things in it, ninety-eight of which I love. The second column had about fifteen things in it, and every one of them was either bland or *blecchh*.

"Somehow I can't work up a whole lot of enthusiasm because I'm allowed to eat all the kale I want."

"Why don't you stop thinking about the food you're not allowed to eat and start thinking about something really important?"

"Like what, for instance?"

"Like Jeff Nugent, for instance."

"How come," I asked, "when you say that all I can think of is Fig Nugents?"

"Cut that out! Look, you're the one who's madly in love with Jeff Nugent. You're the one who—"

"I never said I was madly in love with Jeff Nugent! I said I found him mildly attractive."

"You said—and I quote—'He makes my toes curl.' You said, 'If only I could lose twenty pounds—' "

"You know what, Judy? At this very moment, if you said I could have my choice between Jeff Nugent and a bowl of spaghetti and meatballs, I'd take the spaghetti. It isn't worth it. Not for Jeff Nugent, not for *any* boy."

"What about for yourself?" Judy asked quietly. "Are *you* worth it?"

I hesitated. "I never thought about it that way before."

"Well, think about it. You don't have to lose weight for me to like you. You don't have to lose weight for your parents to love you. And for all I know, you wouldn't have to lose weight for Jeff Nugent to be interested in you. The question is, how do *you* feel about you?"

I didn't answer. The truth was too depressing.

No thin person can ever understand the torture of loving to eat and hating to be fat at the same time. All the circles in my math book reminded me of pizzas. How could I concentrate on my homework when all I wanted to do was draw anchovies and mushrooms on it? Triangles looked like ice cream cones. And it certainly didn't help that half the problems involved *pi,* which equals 3.1416. I kept thinking, "Blueberry *pi* r squared . . . *pi* r squared à la mode."

By dinnertime I thought I was going nuts. (I wasn't allowed to eat them, either.) I went to the kitchen to set the table and looked at the picture of Cheryl Tiegs I had taped to the refrigerator. (The idea was, every time I was tempted to open the refrigerator, I would see thin, gorgeous Cheryl, and that would motivate me to look like her, which I could only do by *not* opening the refrigerator.)

My little brother, Barry, had erased her eyes and drawn little red dots in her eyeballs and fangs sticking out from her mouth.

She still looked better than I did.

We sat down to dinner.

"My, my, doesn't everything look delicious," my father said encouragingly.

"I know what that green guck is and you can't make me eat it," Barry threatened.

"Oh, goody, kale again." I was too weak from hunger to make myself sound as sarcastic as I felt.

"Just because *she's* on a diet," Barry said, "why do *I* have to eat this crummy stuff?"

"It's not crummy stuff," my mother said. "It's healthful, nourishing food. We're all eating more sensibly thanks to Jamie's diet."

"I'm not," said Barry, pushing his plate away, "because I'm not eating."

My father pushed the plate back. "If you don't want to eat the kale, don't eat the kale. But there's nothing wrong with the chicken or the baked potato or the salad."

Barry held his nose. "I can't eat anything with this green gunk all over my plate."

My father jumped up and got a clean plate. "Here," he snapped. He put the chicken and the potato on the clean plate, and took away the one with the kale on it. "Now keep your mouth shut and eat."

"How can I eat with my mouth shut?" Barry asked.

"Barry," my mother warned.

Another pleasant family dinner. "I'm sorry to cause all this trouble," I said softly. "It doesn't seem right for everyone to suffer just because I—"

"First of all, nobody's suffering," my mother said.

"I am," Barry whispered.

"Second of all, you're not causing any trouble. And third of all, even if you were, it's worth it."

Was it?

I looked down at my plate. Even though I was weak from hunger, the sight of a naked baked potato with no butter melting into it, no sour cream oozing over its little bumps and dripping into its little crevices, did nothing to perk me up.

The broiled chicken breast looked nice, but it was so *dry*.

The only thing that was moist or otherwise juicy was the kale.

We won't discuss the kale.

I looked over at my mother's plate. She had butter on her potato. My father had butter *and* sour cream. Barry was mashing his up with butter and a little milk from his glass.

I took a mouthful of dry potato. I washed it down with a sip of 99% fat-free milk.

Is it worth it? I wondered. Judy's question echoed in my mind. Am *I* worth it?

I still didn't have an answer. And what happened the next day didn't make the question any easier.

I was in the supermarket, picking up a few things for my mother. I personally thought that sending a dieter to the supermarket constituted cruelty to fat people, but my mother had to work late and I didn't want to give her a hard time.

I was reaching for a container of fat-free milk when a voice behind me hissed, "Not that one. Take one of these."

I turned around, and there was Jeff Nugent, in a white apron, standing over a plastic crate of milk cartons. He thrust a container at me.

"Jeff! What a—uh—surprise."

Which was putting it mildly. I didn't know whether to be thrilled that I'd run into Jeff like this, or embarrassed because he saw I was buying fat-free milk. I certainly would rather have run into him in the cat food aisle, but we don't have a cat.

I wanted to say, "Oh, this fat-free milk isn't for me, it's for my mother," but that would have been a little obvious. As it was, I couldn't think of a thing to say. Not with him standing so close to me so unexpectedly. My stomach did something funny—and it had nothing to do with hunger.

"See, this is the fresh stuff," Jeff said confidentially. "That stuff on the shelf is going to be outdated in about five minutes."

"Well . . . thanks." I took the container of milk from him. The tips of our fingers touched. The carton slipped out of my hand and fell into the shopping cart. There was a sharp *crack* and several softer crunches as it hit the carton of eggs on the bottom.

"Uh-oh," said Jeff. "I think I broke your eggs."

"No, no, it's my fault."

He reached into my cart and took out the egg carton. Little drips were beginning to seep out the sides. "Shh," he said. He took the eggs down the aisle, picked up another carton, and stuck the broken ones way in the back of the display.

"Well, thanks again," I said as he put the eggs in my cart. There was nothing else I had to get, but I didn't want to leave. I smiled because I couldn't think of anything to say, and he smiled back, sort

of shyly. I think my toes may have curled.

"I—um—didn't know you worked here. I mean, I'm here all the time and I never saw you before." I was babbling, I knew it. Why did I have to say that about being in the supermarket all the time? I could almost hear him thinking, Well, no wonder you're so fat.

"I just started last month," he said. "And I only work from four to nine on school days, so I guess our paths just never crossed before."

How romantic that sounded! Our paths never crossed before . . .

"Did you do the reading for English yet?" he asked. "I didn't even get a chance to look at the assignment, but it sounded like a lot of pages."

"Well, it's just poems, so it's not that much."

Jeff made a face. "Ugh. Ten pages of poems. I hate poetry. I can never understand it."

"It's not so bad. There are pictures on a lot of the pages, so there's not that much to read. But it must be hard, being here till nine and then having to start on homework."

"Yeah, kind of. Especially homework I don't understand." He looked at me sort of shyly. "You're really good in English, aren't you?"

My heart began to thump, and I got this funny tingly sensation on the back of my neck. Was Jeff hinting around, working up to asking me for help in English? Or was he just making conversation? If he was just making conversation, *why?* Why was he standing here talking to me when he should have been unloading milk crates or stacking cottage cheese or raising yogurt prices?

I gripped the handle of my shopping cart hard, hoping that would keep me from showing all I was feeling.

"If you want . . . I mean, I'd be happy to—I mean, if you're having trouble . . ." I just stood there and stammered. And tried to uncurl my toes.

"Would you?" His face lit up. His adorable, sweet, shy face. I was suddenly light-headed, and I knew this wasn't from lack of food either.

"Sure." My voice sounded squeaky. "You could come over after work if you want."

"It wouldn't be too late?" He looked so pleased, so eager, so hopeful. Could he be *that* excited about getting help with the assignment? Or was that look on his face because *I* was going to give him the help?

But how could that be? How could Jeff Nugent, the cute, want to snuggle up to Jamie Wade, the plump, and discuss Robert Browning (the poet)?

Maybe, I thought wildly, my diet has worked already. Maybe I'm not fat anymore.

". . . yeah, nine-fifteen's okay. See you then."

Dazed, I checked out my stuff, practically sprinted home, and ran upstairs to weigh myself.

I'd lost one pound.

Could one pound have made that much of a difference?

"It's crazy," I told Judy on the phone. "He *does* like me. I mean, he's been here four times and we only spend about fifteen minutes on the homework. The rest of the time we just talk. I mean, I really think he likes me."

"I think he does, too," said Judy. "It sure sounds like it. So what's so crazy about that?"

"He wasn't supposed to like me until I lost twenty pounds. What does he see in me?"

"What do you mean, what does he see in you? You're nice, you're fun, you have a good personality—and twenty pounds overweight is not exactly like being an elephant, you know. Don't look a gift horse in the mouth."

"I wish you'd stop talking about meat," I sighed.

"Still hungry?"

"I'm *always* hungry. You know, it's a myth that being in love takes away your appetite."

"Yeah?" Judy laughed. "Remember when you said if you had a choice between Jeff and a bowl of spaghetti, you'd take the spaghetti? Would you still take the spaghetti? . . . Jamie?

Jamie? Didn't you hear what I said?"

"I'm thinking, I'm *thinking*."

I didn't have to make a choice.

The next week Jeff suggested we go to the movies. And after the movie we stopped at McDonald's. I hesitated only a second before deciding that a Big Mac and a thick shake were just what I needed.

I took one bite of the Big Mac and one sip of the shake and fell off my diet with a crash. I'll make up for it tomorrow, I told myself. I won't eat a thing tomorrow. Or Monday either. I know there are five million calories in a Big Mac and ten million in a thick shake. So I won't eat Tuesday.

But at that moment, with that first ambrosial taste of gloppy sauce and pickle and lettuce, with that first nectar sip of a thick shake . . . it was heaven. Of course, food always tastes better when you eat it with someone you love.

Especially if you've been starving for ten days.

On Sunday, Jeff asked if I wanted to go to the nature preserve at the state park. How romantic, I thought, walking through a deserted forest of bare trees in November, just the two of us . . .

It was wonderful. Jeff casually took my hand in his, and when the wind picked up he sort of held me against him so I wouldn't be blown away. I was hardly thin enough yet to be blown away—especially after last night's binge—but maybe Jeff saw me that way. Maybe I didn't look as heavy to him as I did to myself.

You know, you can work up a whale of an appetite walking for miles through a deserted forest in November. The way I figured it, I must have walked off at least a million of the calories I'd taken in last night, so when Jeff wanted to stop to get something to eat, I agreed enthusiastically.

After all that good exercise, I hardly felt guilty about wolfing down my fish and chips. (Fried. Both on the "Forbidden" list.)

I spent the rest of the day alternating between moods. After Jeff dropped me off at home, I mooned around my room for about half an hour, replaying the soft kiss he'd given me at the preserve, just before we went for fish and chips.

Then, for the next hour, I hated myself for eating the fish and chips. I felt guilty, stupid, weak.

Which made me hungry.

I went downstairs to the kitchen and yanked the refrigerator door open. I looked inside, then slammed it shut. I glared at the picture of Cheryl Tiegs. I imagined I saw reproach in her eyes. (Which was silly, because all she had in her eyes were those little red pinpoints that Barry had drawn.)

"Jamie," I could hear her saying, "how could you? Don't you want to look like me?"

I ripped the picture off the refrigerator door.

"Why should I want to look like you? Jeff likes me just the way I am. He doesn't care if I lose twenty pounds or not. And the only reason I started this stupid diet in the first place was because I thought he'd notice me and like me if I was thin. Well, I'm not thin and he likes me, anyway. So I don't have to lose weight for Jeff."

And then, eerily, I sort of imagined Cheryl's

voice and Judy's voice blending together, and this combined voice said, "What about for you, Jamie? What about for yourself?"

"You know," I told Judy on the phone, "it's very hard to diet and to be in love at the same time."

"You mean, you still can't decide whether to dream about Jeff or spaghetti?"

"Well, sort of. But what it really is . . . every time I think about Jeff I can't help thinking about all that food I eat when I go out with him. So I start to feel guilty and then I start hating myself and then I can't think about Jeff anymore."

"Sounds to me like what you really mean is it's hard to be in love and *not* diet. If you stuck to your diet, you wouldn't feel guilty and hate yourself, and you could dream about Jeff all you wanted."

"If I stuck to my diet I'd probably be too hungry to dream about Jeff. I'd be dreaming about hot fudge sundaes. And besides, I don't want him to know I'm on a diet."

"The way you're eating now, he'll never know, that's for sure."

"Thanks a lot," I said sourly.

"But why would he have to know?"

"What am I going to say if he asks if I want a Big Mac?"

"How about 'no thanks.' Or is that too simple?"

"But what if he asks how come? I mean, all of a sudden I don't like Big Macs?"

"Tell him you're not hungry."

"Listen, Judy," I said bitterly, "a good relationship is not built on lies."

I struggled through the rest of the week battling hunger pangs. I was back on my diet again, but it didn't seem to be any easier. I tried substituting thoughts of Jeff kissing me for thoughts of spaghetti, french fries, and devil's food cake, but it didn't work too well. As I saw it, the problem was that I knew I could have my devil's food cake and Jeff, too.

But for some reason, I felt this determination to stick to my "Permitted Foods" list. Maybe it was like punishing myself for the binge I'd had over the weekend, but whatever the reason, by the time Jeff and I went out again the next Saturday, I'd lost three pounds. (I was sure it would have been four if I hadn't slipped off the wagon.)

We went to a party at one of Jeff's friend's houses, and along with the usual potato chips and stuff there was this huge, five-foot-long hero sandwich. You just cut off a piece for yourself whenever you get hungry.

I looked at it longingly. There were all kinds of good things in there. Cold cuts, cheese, olives, peppers, onions . . .

After we'd danced a couple of times, Jeff said, "Let's have some of that sandwich. I'm really starving."

I looked at the hero and I looked up at Jeff. Even slow dancing works up an appetite—well,

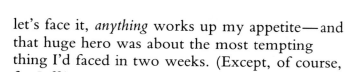

Five-Foot

let's face it, *anything* works up my appetite—and that huge hero was about the most tempting thing I'd faced in two weeks. (Except, of course, for Jeff.)

"Isn't that a great idea?" he said. "A five-foot hero sandwich? Only, it's not five feet anymore. I think there's only about two feet left. Come on, Jamie, I'll cut us off a couple of pieces."

Oh, why not? I asked myself. It's a party. It's special. Just this once. I'll make up for it tomorrow. I won't eat a thing tomorrow. How often do I get a chance to help demolish a five-foot hero sandwich?

"No," I said, before I even realized I was going to say it. "No thanks, Jeff. You go ahead and get a piece for yourself."

"You sure?" he asked doubtfully.

I'm sure that I made those same excuses for gorging last week. I'm sure that I'll hate myself if I eat so much as a mouthful of that sandwich, just as I hated myself all week for the Big Mac and the fish and chips. I don't want to hate myself anymore.

"Yeah, I'm sure."

Hero Sandwich

Jeff came back with a big chunk of the sandwich. "It's fantastic," he said. "Here, try a bite."

I turned my head away quickly, before I could get a good whiff of the strong cheese, the pungent peppers, the fragrant oil . . .

"I can't, Jeff," I said bluntly. "I'm on a diet."

"On a diet? What for?"

"To lose weight. I have seventeen pounds to go."

"I mean, why do you have to lose weight?"

"Oh, come on, Jeff," I said impatiently. "I'm twenty pounds overweight. At least, I was. Don't pretend you didn't notice."

"I'm not pretending *anything*. I like you just the way you are."

"Oh, Jeff . . . that's such a nice thing to say." I felt my heart melting and hoped it didn't mean my determination was melting, too.

"I'm not just saying it. It's the truth. To me you look . . ." He hesitated a moment, then said shyly, ". . . really good." He took a big bite of his hero and chewed hard.

"But to me I don't."

That was it, I realized. That was it in a nutshell. Jeff may like me just the way I am, but I don't. And I didn't want to hate myself anymore. Not for the way I ate, not for the way I looked.

I wasn't losing twenty pounds for Jeff, or for the doctor, or for my mother or for anyone except myself. I knew the answer to Judy's question now. I'd probably really known it all the time.

"You're the one that counts," Jeff said. "If it's important to you, that's what matters. I think it's great you have that much will power."

"Oh, Jeff, I don't!" I wailed. "It's so hard. I mean, right this minute I want to rip that sandwich out of your hands and wolf the whole thing down before you can grab it back."

Jeff grinned. "You just try it, Jamie. Just try it."

"You wouldn't let me?"

"Not if you don't want me to. You helped me with poetry, didn't you?"

"You mean, you'll help me with my diet?"

"If it's what you want," he said, "I'll help you any way I can."

"Oh, Jeff." I looked into his eyes. He was gazing down at me so gravely, so intently, I forgot all about hero sandwiches and potato chips and stupid, unimportant things.

I sighed.

"Oh, my," I murmured. "I think you're helping me already."

Thinking About It

1. A voice says to Jamie, "What about for yourself?" Think of a time when you had to decide whether to do something for yourself or for others. What helped you make your decision?

2. Do friends help or hinder Jamie from becoming the person she wants to be? What can you cite in the story to support your answer?

3. A theme of the story could be summed up something like this: "Be true to yourself; you're the one you have to be with the rest of your life." Think of four or five other lessons from your own experience that could be included in a "Teen Guide to the Rest of Your Life."

EARL J. DIAS

BASED ON THE STORY BY GUY DE MAUPASSANT

The Necklace

Characters

MATHILDE LOISEL   CHARLES LOISEL   RENAULT
CECILE FORESTIER   MADAME GROUET   LISETTE

Scene 1 ᨐᨕᨒ

TIME: *A January evening.*

SETTING: *The Loisel apartment in Paris. The room is shabby and the furniture is old and worn. Table at center is set for two; there is a large soup plate at each place, and a loaf of French bread in the center of the table.*

AT RISE: **MATHILDE LOISEL** *sits at the table, and* **CECILE FORESTIER** *sits in an armchair.*

CECILE: To think, Mathilde, that I have seen you only twice since our school days. That is why I took the liberty of dropping by today.

MATHILDE: I'm glad you did, Cecile. It is pleasant to see you. (*Looking around room*) But you can see why I do not invite any of my old school friends here. This is scarcely a palace, and certainly not the kind of luxury you are accustomed to.

CECILE: You deserve better, Mathilde—a girl as beautiful as you. (*She smiles.*) Do you remember how you used to dream?

MATHILDE (*Bitterly*): I remember. I used to hope that some day I would live in a huge mansion. I'd have vestibules hung with Oriental tapestries and lighted by tall lamps of bronze. (*Laughing wryly*) I was to have large parlors decked with old silk, and, oh, yes, coquettish little rooms, prepared and perfumed for a five o'clock chit-chat with intimate friends. (*She shrugs her shoulders.*) So, here I am.

CECILE: And your husband, Charles. How is he?

MATHILDE: Charles means well. He is good-hearted and does his best, but the salary of a minor clerk in the Ministry of Education is not much.

CECILE: You could have done better. Do you remember how much the Marquis de Montfleury was taken with you? He used to send you flowers.

MATHILDE (*Dreamily*): Ah, the Marquis. He was so slim, so elegant, so charming. (*She sighs in resignation.*) But he was not for me—a poor girl with no dowry to offer. So my parents did the best they could for me by arranging my marriage to Charles.

CECILE: And a lucky man he is to have won himself such a beauty.

MATHILDE: Beauty? (*Gestures around room*) What is it in these surroundings? All my life I have dreamed of dining in famous restaurants—Maxim's, Fouquet's—of dancing among the rich, and well, you see where I am. What have I to look forward to?

CECILE (*Rising and coming to her*): My poor Mathilde.

MATHILDE: The least I can do is to offer you a cup of tea.

CECILE: No. Thank you, but I must be on my way.

Marcel and I are dining tonight with the Count de Guiche.

MATHILDE: How I envy you. (*Bitterly*) Charles and I are dining here as you can see. (**CHARLES LOISEL** *enters, with newspaper under his arm.*)

CHARLES: Good evening, Mathilde. (*Surprised*) Why, Madame Forestier! I have not seen you in many months.

CECILE: (*Shaking* **CHARLES**'s *hand*): How do you do, Monsieur Loisel.

CHARLES: I am glad you paid us a visit. Mathilde is alone a good deal. Will you stay to eat with us?

MATHILDE (*Quickly*): Cecile has a dinner engagement, Charles.

CHARLES: That is too bad. Perhaps another time.

CECILE: Of course, another time. But now I must go. We must see each other soon, Mathilde. There is no reason for us to be strangers.

MATHILDE (*Accompanying her to door*): Yes, we will meet again soon. (**MATHILDE** *and* **CECILE** *exit.* **CHARLES** *sits at table, tucks napkin under his chin, unfolds newspaper and begins to read. After a moment,* **MATHILDE** *re-enters.*)

CHARLES: Madame Forestier looks most prosperous.

MATHILDE: As well she should. Her husband has one of the great fortunes in France.

CHARLES: Lucky fellow.

MATHILDE: Lucky woman.

CHARLES: I am devilishly hungry tonight. This winter air gives a man an appetite.

MATHILDE (*Dully*): I'll get the meal. (**CHARLES** *continues to read the newspaper.* **MATHILDE** *exits and then returns with a tureen of soup. She ladles soup into* **CHARLES**'s *plate.* **CHARLES** *puts newspaper aside.*)

CHARLES (*Breaking off piece of bread from loaf and sniffing his plate*): Ah, the good soup!

MATHILDE (*Ladling soup into her own plate and then speaking ironically*): Ah, yes, the good soup. (*She places tureen on table and sits.* **CHARLES** *eats his soup eagerly, dipping his bread into plate.* **MATHILDE**, *watching him rather distastefully, eats more delicately.*)

CHARLES: This soup has a fine flavor—as good as my mother used to make. (*Mops his plate with bread*) The kind of meal that sticks to a man's ribs.

MATHILDE: Would you like more?

CHARLES: All in good time, but first I have a surprise for you.

MATHILDE: A surprise?

CHARLES: Something that should please you very much. (*He takes envelope from his pocket, opens it and draws out a card.*) Listen. (*Reading; importantly*) "The Minister of Education and Madame Georges Ramponeau request the honor of M. and Mme. Loisel's presence at the Place of the Ministry on Monday, January 18." (*Proudly*) Now, what do you think of that, Mathilde?

MATHILDE: What do you expect me to think of that?

CHARLES (*Bewildered*): But, my dear, I thought you would be pleased. You never go out, and here's a chance—a fine one. These invitations are greatly sought after, and not many are given to the clerks. Everyone in the official world will be at this party.

MATHILDE (*Impatiently*): What do you expect me to wear?

CHARLES: Why, the dress in which you go to the theater. That looks very pretty to me. (**MATHILDE** *puts her face in her hands and begins to sob.* **CHARLES** *is very surprised.*) What is the

matter, Mathilde? Why are you crying?

MATHILDE (*Controlling herself; wiping tears from her cheek*): I have no clothes to wear to this party. Give your invitation to some colleague whose wife has a better outfit than I. (**CHARLES** *looks hurt. He frowns, then speaks hesitantly.*)

CHARLES: See here, Mathilde—how much would a simple dress cost? Something that would do on other occasions, too?

MATHILDE (*Hesitating*): I—I don't know, exactly. (*Frowns*) But it seems to me that four hundred francs might do.

CHARLES (*Alarmed*): Four hundred francs! (*He shakes his head. Then, as* **MATHILDE**'s *face falls, he continues quickly.*) Still, we might do it. I had been saving for a gun. I thought I might do some shooting at Nanterre next summer, but this is more important. (*Firmly*) Yes, you shall have the four hundred francs. (*Forcing a smile*) But take care to buy a pretty dress.

MATHILDE: Oh, Charles! (*She jumps up, comes to* **CHARLES,** *and kisses him on the cheek.*) How generous you are! And I assure you it will be a pretty dress. (*She frowns suddenly.*) But no, it is really impossible.

CHARLES: Impossible? Why?

MATHILDE: The women at the Ministry will not only be beautifully dressed but will wear handsome jewels as well. (*She returns to her place at the table.*) It annoys me not to have a jewel, not a single stone to put on. I shall look dreadful.

CHARLES: You can wear some natural flowers. They are very stylish this time of year. For ten francs, you can get two or three magnificent roses.

MATHILDE (*Shaking her head*): No, there's nothing more humiliating than to look poor among a lot of rich women.

CHARLES: But, Mathilde, I'm afraid I cannot help you there. The dress, yes, but jewelry is beyond our reach.

MATHILDE: That is just what I have been telling you. (CHARLES *stares moodily at his plate.* MATHILDE *toys with a piece of bread. Suddenly,* CHARLES *bangs the table.*)

CHARLES: I have it! Why did I not think of it before? Your friend, Madame Forestier.

MATHILDE: What about her?

CHARLES: Ask her to lend you some jewelry. She has plenty. Why, she was wearing a ring with a diamond as big as an onion. She likes you. I am sure she would let you borrow some bauble or other.

MATHILDE (*Musing*): That's true. I had not thought of it. (*Coming to life*) What a wonderful idea, Charles! (*Rising*) I shall go to her house at once. I'm sure I can catch her before she leaves for dinner at the Count's.

CHARLES (*Relieved*): Good. I'll clean up here while you're gone.

MATHILDE (*Happily*): It will be a splendid party, will it not, Charles?

CHARLES: You will be the most beautiful woman there.

MATHILDE: I hope so. But now I must get dressed and run. (*She exits hurriedly.* **CHARLES** *rises, sighs, shrugs his shoulders, and begins to carry the plates from the table as the curtains close.*)

Scene 2 ⤸

TIME: *A few days later; the day of the party.*

SETTING: *Same as Scene 1.*

AT RISE: **CHARLES,** *wearing a suit, sits at table. He draws his watch from his pocket, looks at it, and shakes his head.*

CHARLES (*Loudly*): Mathilde! Are you ready? We should be there by eight.

MATHILDE (*Offstage*): Coming, Charles. (*After a moment or two,* **MATHILDE,** *wearing a lovely gown, appears in doorway and poses for a moment. She holds a necklace.*) How do I look?

CHARLES (*Rising and gazing at her admiringly*): You are more beautiful than ever, Mathilde.

MATHILDE: Now you shall see what I borrowed from Cecile. I did not show it to you before because I wished to surprise you. (*She displays the necklace.*) Look. Is it not lovely?

CHARLES: It is magnificent!

MATHILDE: Help me clasp it around my neck. (**CHARLES** *does so.*)

CHARLES (*Standing off to look at her*): Perfect!

MATHILDE (*Posing happily*): You see, it is simple but expensive looking. Oh, I thought for a long time before I chose it, Charles. Cecile has such a collection of jewelry; I was tempted by all of it. Bracelets, a pearl necklace, a Venetian cross of gold set with precious stones. I tried on all of them and posed before the glass. And then I discovered in a box of satin this superb necklace of diamonds. I was in ecstasy when I put it on.

CHARLES: It was a wise choice, my dear.

MATHILDE: And now I shall get my wrap, and I will be ready. (*Happily doing a little pirouette*) Oh, Charles, it will be a wonderful evening—one of the great nights of our lives. (*They exit. The lights are dimmed or the curtains close briefly to denote the passage of time.*)

Scene 3 ೕ⌒ೋ

TIME: *A few hours later.*

SETTING: *Same as Scene 2.*

AT RISE: CHARLES *and* MATHILDE *enter.* MATHILDE *is in high spirits, but* CHARLES *seems tired.*

MATHILDE: What a glorious party!

CHARLES (*Sinking wearily into chair*): You certainly were a success, Mathilde. (*Wryly*) After midnight, I just retired to the anteroom with three other men whose wives were also having a good time.

MATHILDE: I danced with everyone—all the most distinguished men! The Count de Brisaille, the Marquis Saint-Challet, Monsieur Deveau— even the Minister himself.

CHARLES (*Wearily*): So I observed. All the men were looking at you, inquiring your name, and asking to be introduced.

MATHILDE (*Dancing gracefully around the room*): I shall never be able to sleep tonight. I am on a cloud of happiness.

CHARLES (*Yawning*): As for me, I shall sleep like a log. This night life is too much for me.

MATHILDE: Charles, how can you say that? Tonight

was life as it should be — glittering, romantic, joyful.

CHARLES (*Stifling another yawn*): That may be. But take off your wrap, my dear. It is rather warm in here. (**MATHILDE** *removes her wrap, throws it onto the table, continues to dance, and then stops suddenly, her hand at her neck. She utters a startled cry.*)

CHARLES (*Alarmed*): What is it?

MATHILDE (*Terrified*): The necklace! I don't have it!

CHARLES (*Jumping up*): It must be somewhere. (*Picks up wrap*) Perhaps in the folds of your wrap. (*He searches intently.*) No, it is not here.

MATHILDE (*Disturbed*): Look in your coat pocket, Charles. Perhaps I gave it to you.

CHARLES: No, I am sure you did not. But let us see. (*He turns his pockets inside out.*) No, nothing. (*He goes toward door.*) Perhaps you dropped it on the stairs. I shall look. (*He exits hurriedly.* **MATHILDE** *begins to look frantically around the room — under the table, under chairs — then looks again in the folds of her wrap. She wrings her hands in distress.*) Oh, where could it be? (*After a moment,* **CHARLES** *re-enters.*)

MATHILDE (*Hopefully*): Did you find it?

CHARLES (*Shaking head*): Not a trace. It is not on

the stairs. And I was lucky because the cab we came in is still outside. The driver is feeding his horse. The necklace is not in the cab.

MATHILDE (*Miserably*): What are we to do?

CHARLES: Are you sure you had it when we left the party?

MATHILDE: Yes. I touched it in the vestibule of the Ministry.

CHARLES: Perhaps it will turn up, but I fear we are out of luck, Mathilde. The chances are you dropped it on the street. And the streets of Paris being what they are, I doubt if anyone who finds so valuable a necklace will even report it to the police.

MATHILDE: Why did this have to happen? Does fate begrudge us one night of pleasure?

CHARLES: I do not know about fate, Mathilde. But I know that we must do something about this. First of all, you must write to Madame Forestier. Tell her that you have broken the clasp of her necklace and that you are having it repaired. That will give us more time to search for it.

MATHILDE (*Eagerly*): Yes, I will do that at once. (*She exits quickly and returns in a moment with paper, pen, and ink, which she places on table.*)

CHARLES: If the necklace does not turn up, we must, of course, replace it.

MATHILDE: Replace it? But, Charles, the necklace must be worth a fortune.

CHARLES: I *know* it is worth a fortune. There is a jeweler's shop in the Palais Royal not far from the Ministry. I pass it every day. In the window is a necklace that is almost an exact replica of the one you borrowed from Madame Forestier. There is a price tag on it.

MATHILDE (*Eagerly*): And the cost?

CHARLES: Forty thousand francs.

MATHILDE (*In dismay*): Forty thousand francs! We could never afford it.

CHARLES: If the other is not found, we must afford it. After all, Mathilde, I may not have much money, but I pride myself on being an honest man.

MATHILDE: But forty thousand francs!

CHARLES: I have, as you know, eighteen thousand francs which my father left me. I have never touched it. That can be a start.

MATHILDE: And the rest?

CHARLES: We must borrow it.

MATHILDE: But, Charles, we shall then be in the hands of the moneylenders. You remember what happened when Monsieur LeBreque's business failed. He borrowed, asking a thousand francs here, five hundred there, a few louis elsewhere. He gave promissory notes, made ruinous agreements, dealt with usurers. When he died, he was living in poverty, and still paying.

CHARLES: I know. But what would you have us do? Do you want to go to Madame Forestier and say, "I'm sorry, Cecile, but a little accident happened. I lost your forty-thousand-franc necklace. Ha! Ha! These things will happen, won't they?"

MATHILDE (*Tearfully*): You are being cruel, Charles.

CHARLES: Not cruel, Mathilde—honest. One has to face the troubles that come in life. (*More gently*) Come now, Mathilde. Write that note to Madame Forestier. I will mail it before I go to bed. (**MATHILDE** *takes up her pen, thinks for a moment, and then begins to write.* **CHARLES** *sits staring* *thoughtfully into space. Suddenly, **MATHILDE** stops writing, puts her head down on table, and begins to sob. **CHARLES** looks at her for a moment, then rises and comes to her, putting his hand on her shoulder.*)

CHARLES: There! There! We will meet this together. (*She continues to sob. He pats her shoulder, stares in front of him, and shakes his head.*) What a little thing it takes to save you or to ruin you. (*Curtain*)

Scene 4 ❦

TIME: *Ten years later.*

SETTING: *The Loisels' attic room, in the Paris slums. The only furniture is a battered old table and three or four rickety wooden chairs.*

AT RISE: MATHILDE, *mop in hand, is washing the floor, a bucket of water by her side. She looks much older, has a red face, and there are traces of gray in her hair. Her sleeves are rolled to her elbows and she wears a dirty apron. Children's voices are heard shouting outside. **MATHILDE** looks irritated, goes to the window, and yells in a loud and coarse voice.*

MATHILDE: Shut your mouths down there, you street rats! You get noisier every day! Can't one get at least a little peace and quiet in this wreck of a neighborhood? Go home to your mothers—if you have any! (*The children's voices die away.* **MATHILDE** *returns to center and resumes mopping.*) Noisy brats! (**CHARLES** *enters. He looks tired, seedy, and much older. He is carrying a ledger.*)

CHARLES (*Yawning*): I was up all night with these accounts. I tell you, Mathilde, to work all day at my own job and then to do accounts on the side for the little money they bring in is almost too much.

MATHILDE (*Harshly*): You should be used to it by now. We've had ten years of this miserable life.

CHARLES: At least our debts are finally paid.

MATHILDE: Oh, yes, our debts are paid. (*Bitterly*) And look at me. Is this the Mathilde you married?

CHARLES (*Wearily*): We have both changed. Time changes us all. (*Sighing*) Well, I must be off to the Ministry. I'll be lucky if I can keep my eyes open. (*He exits.*)

MADAME GROUET (*Offstage*): Vegetables! Vegetables for sale!

MATHILDE (*Going to window and speaking coarsely*): Come up! Let us see what garbage you are peddling this morning! (*After a moment,* MADAME GROUET *enters. She carries a basket of cabbages and carrots.*)

MADAME GROUET: Bonjour, Madame Loisel. I have some lovely vegetables today.

MATHILDE: You've been saying that for ten years, Madame Grouet, and your vegetables get worse each year. (*Taking a cabbage from basket and feeling it*) Ugh! This cabbage is old enough to be your grandmother.

MADAME GROUET: But, madame, I swear it was picked fresh this morning.

MATHILDE (*Fingering carrots*): And these carrots are loaded with worms.

MADAME GROUET: But no, madame—they are

jewels of carrots.

MATHILDE: How much for this grandmother cabbage?

MADAME GROUET: Twenty sous.

MATHILDE (*Throwing cabbage back into basket*): Take your basket and sell your wares to the other fools in the neighborhood, you old fraud. Twenty sous! Why, you old robber, it is not worth ten.

MADAME GROUET: Please, madame, at twenty sous it is an immense bargain.

MATHILDE (*Turning her back on* **MADAME GROUET**): Do you think I'm a lunatic?

MADAME GROUET: Madame is unkind. (*Slyly*) But I will offer you a real bargain. You may have the cabbage for fifteen sous.

MATHILDE (*Beginning to mop again and getting the mop close to* **MADAME GROUET**'s *feet*): Be off with you!

MADAME GROUET (*Trying to avoid the mop*): But it is a great bargain.

MATHILDE (*Stopping her work and leaning on the mop*): I'll give you twelve sous. No more.

MADAME GROUET: Ah, madame drives a hard bargain. But one must live. It is yours madame, for twelve sous.

MATHILDE: And robbery at that. (**MATHILDE** *puts the cabbage on the table, then takes a worn purse from her apron pocket and counts out twelve coins, one by one, into* **MADAME GROUET**'s *hand.*)

MADAME GROUET: Ah, thank you, madame. You will find that cabbage to be the king of all cabbages. Delicious. Mouth-watering.

MATHILDE: Save the speeches for the other poor fools you deal with. Get out. I'm busy.

(**MADAME GROUET** *exits quickly as* **MATHILDE** *begins to mop furiously once more. She speaks to herself as* *she works.*) Ah, what a miserable life! I work all day and eat rotten vegetables at night!

RENAULT (*Offstage*): Beef! Veal! Freshly killed chickens! (MATHILDE *stops mopping, smiles grimly, exits, and returns with a paper bag, which she places on table. Then she goes right and yells.*)

MATHILDE: Monsieur Renault! Come up!

RENAULT: Oui, madame! At once! (RENAULT *enters, wearing a stained butcher's apron and carrying a basket.*)

RENAULT: Bonjour, Madame Loisel. I have here a piece of veal to end all pieces of veal. Young, tender—the dew is still on it.

MATHILDE (*Taking paper bag from table and shaking it in his face*): Listen, you old goat. I have here a piece of beef you sold me yesterday.

RENAULT: Yes, I remember. A magnificent cut. Fit for a king.

MATHILDE (*Throwing the bag at him*): It's as tough as rope. I cooked it all day, and we still couldn't eat it. And for this gristle, you charged me fifty sous, you old crook!

RENAULT (*Picking up bag*): But, madame, there must be some mistake.

MATHILDE: There is—and you made it! I want my fifty sous back!

RENAULT: But that is not good business, madame. I sold you the meat in good faith.

MATHILDE (*Advancing with the mop and shaking it at him*): I want my fifty sous!

RENAULT (*Retreating and speaking coaxingly*): But, madame, that is not business. (*She again shakes the mop at him.*) Let me do this. I will give you this piece of oh-so-tender veal in exchange for the beef. This will prove I am an honest man.

MATHILDE (*Angrily*): You don't have an honest bone

A · 103

in your body! I want my fifty sous.

RENAULT: Very well, madame. (*He reaches into his pocket and gives* MATHILDE *some money. She counts the coins carefully.*)

MATHILDE (*Looking up*): You robber! There are only forty-eight sous here!

RENAULT: Forty-eight? (*He looks carefully at the coins in* MATHILDE's *hand.*) But, of course. I made a mistake in counting. (*He gives* MATHILDE *two sous more.*) There. Again I prove I am an honest man.

MATHILDE: Ha! That's the best joke I've heard today.

RENAULT: But now about this veal, madame. You have my word for it—it is an exquisite cut. From a prize calf, no less. (*He takes a bag from his basket, holds it up.*) And at the unbelievably low price of fifty-five sous. Reduced from sixty, just for you, madame.

MATHILDE: That veal would probably break whatever teeth I have left.

RENAULT: But, madame, I swear on my honor—

MATHILDE (*Advancing on him and shaking the mop at him*): Get out! I've had enough of your tricks for one day!

RENAULT (*Retreating*): But the veal—

MATHILDE: This is for the veal! (*She takes a vicious swipe at him with the mop, and he exits hurriedly.* MATHILDE *goes to table, sits, and counts the fifty sous again. She begins to laugh robustly.* LISETTE, *a girl of 15, enters.*)

LISETTE: You seem happy, Madame Loisel.

MATHILDE: When one outwits a thief, one has a right to be happy. What do you want, Lisette?

LISETTE: There is a woman out there who has been asking for you.

MATHILDE: What does she look like?

LISETTE: She is very pretty, and she is wearing

the loveliest dress.

MATHILDE: Well, when you see her, tell her to come up. Anyone dressed well will be a welcome change in this neighborhood of scarecrows. Were you one of the brats making all that noise a while ago?

LISETTE: Oh, no, Madame Loisel. I have been taking my music lesson.

MATHILDE: Well, see that you don't hang around with that noisy bunch.

LISETTE (*Meekly*): Yes, madame. (*She goes to door.*) I'll tell the lady she may come up when she wishes.

MATHILDE (*Unconcernedly*): Suit yourself. It's all the same to me. (**LISETTE** *exits*. **MATHILDE** *resumes her mopping. After a moment or two,* **CECILE FORESTIER** *enters.*)

CECILE: Oh, I am sorry. There must be some mistake. I was looking for Madame Loisel. (**MATHILDE** *looks up, is surprised, and smiles.*)

MATHILDE: Good morning, Cecile.

CECILE: But, madame, I do not know you. Are you not making a mistake? (**MATHILDE** *goes to her, takes her hand, and leads her to center.*)

MATHILDE: There is no mistake, Cecile. I am Mathilde Loisel.

CECILE (*Gazing closely at her and uttering a startled cry*): Oh! My poor Mathilde! How you have changed!

MATHILDE: Yes, I have had hard days since I last saw you. And many troubles—all because of you.

CECILE: Because of me? How so? It is at least ten years since I have seen you.

MATHILDE: You remember the diamond necklace that you lent me to wear to the ball at the Ministry?

CECILE: Yes. What of it?

MATHILDE: Well, I lost it.

CECILE: But how can that be? You brought it back to me soon after the ball.

MATHILDE: I brought you back another just like it— one that cost forty thousand francs. And now for ten years Charles and I have been paying for it. You must understand that it was not easy for us who had nothing. At last, our debt is paid off, and I am very glad.

CECILE (*After a long pause*): You—you say that you bought a diamond necklace to replace mine?

MATHILDE (*Smiling proudly*): Yes. You did not even notice it, did you? They were exactly alike!
(CECILE *looks desolate and sadly shakes her head. Much moved, she takes both of* MATHILDE's *hands.* MATHILDE *looks questioningly at her.*) Cecile, what is the matter?

CECILE: Oh, my poor Mathilde! (*She pauses.*) The necklace that I lent you was false. It was only a paste imitation. (MATHILDE *looks horrified.*) At most, it was worth five hundred francs.
(MATHILDE *looks even more stunned. She sways as though about to faint as* CECILE *grasps her and the curtains close quickly.*)

Thinking About It

1. "If only I had known!" How does this statement apply to the play, and how does it apply to you?

2. What if Madame Loisel had not lost the necklace? Would she have been happy? What details in the play helped you answer?

3. Many stories, movies, or TV programs have surprise endings. Think of one such example other than *The Necklace* and tell your classmates about it. Why do you think we enjoy such endings?

ALICE CALAPRICE

BASED ON A DIARY BY BERND HEINRICH

Nature's Notebook

from AN OWL IN THE HOUSE

Preface

A few years ago I did something that I probably shouldn't have done, but to my mind I didn't have much of a choice, really. I adopted a wild animal—a baby great horned owl—after I found it buried in the snow in the Vermont woods near my home.

I am a zoologist and a naturalist. That means I study animals that live in the wild. I know very well that wild animals should usually be left to fend for themselves, and that many die an early death in the process. This is the way nature intended it to be. It is unkind to force a wild animal into captivity. Tampering with nature's ways causes the natural system of interdependence of all wild animals and plants to become unbalanced. In addition, most wild animals die when they leave their natural habitat and food supply. Despite this knowledge, I felt a moment of kinship with the owlet and instinctively reached out to protect it. I could not leave it there to die.

Most wild animals are protected by government agencies, and it is illegal to take them as pets. But I knew that, because I am a scientist, I could get permission to keep the owl and to study its development. I was very curious about how a docile owlet develops into a large and fierce predator; I was also curious about how this owl would interact with human beings.

Male and female owlets look alike, so for no particular reason I decided to refer to this one as "he." I named him Bubo, which is part of his scientific name, *Bubo virginianus*. Bubo became very special to me, and I think I was special to him.

I decided to keep a diary of Bubo's growth and development. Field biologists call such a diary a "field notebook"; in it they keep a record of their observations, speculate about what may be going on with the animal's behavior, and sometimes express their feelings at the moment of observation. I wanted to do all of that with Bubo. I knew I would have to teach him to fend for himself, but I had a hunch that he would have much more to teach me—about himself, about great horned owls in general, and probably even about myself.   *Camp Kaflunk, Maine*
November 1986

By mid–March in northern Vermont, the snow from the winter storms is already beginning to thaw during the day, but the cold nights still produce a hard white crust on the ground. The warmer temperatures are beginning to trigger the flow of sap from the sugar maples, and you can feel that spring is just around the corner.

From where I stood at the edge of the thick woods overlooking Shelburne Bog, I felt a cold breeze pushing in from the north. Eerie creaking, scraping, and moaning sounds invaded the forest. The sky was turning dark, and the woods were growing pitch-black. Above the wind, I heard a booming, resonating "hoo-hoo-*hooo*-hoo!" To me it was a friendly sound, for I knew it was the call of a great horned owl.

When I returned to the same woods in early April, the signs of spring were more abundant. Some flowers were beginning to pop through the damp brown forest floor, birds were starting to build their nests, and the first spring peepers were calling out from the pond. In the dusk, I briefly saw a dark silhouette glide silently over the pines. I knew instantly that it was a large owl, maybe the one I had heard the month before. It vanished behind the pines, but not from my mind. I returned again on April 17, hoping to see the owl once more. And sure enough, through the thick evergreen branches I caught a glimpse of a large owl with ear tufts—a great horned owl. For a moment, our eyes met, and then the big bird turned its head and launched itself over the darkening forest.

Of all the owls, the great horned owl is the supreme predator. Among the predatory birds of North America, it is exceeded in weight only by eagles. This awesome bird has been called the "winged tiger"; but as I watched it glide quietly through the dusk, it did not seem savage at all.

I was curious to know if an owl's nest might be out there, so I set out to search for it before

nightfall. I came across the nests of various birds, but one in particular caught my attention. I recognized the nest as a crow's nest, but that made no difference; great horned owls have never learned to build nests, so they use either large tree hollows or nests already built by crows, hawks, ravens, or other large birds. But crows, for instance, clean up the droppings of their young, and I noticed that whitewash splotched some of the branches. Then I noticed bird pellets on the forest floor. These are hard, dry, oval-shaped balls of fur, feathers, bones, and insect remains that owls (and some other birds) can't digest, so they cough them up, or "regurgitate" them. There is a mystery behind each pellet, and some people like to open them up to see what's inside. You can often tell what the bird ate, and from that you try to guess what kind of bird it may have been. If, for example, a pellet contains the remains of a rodent, it is probably an owl or hawk pellet. When I opened one of the pellets, I recognized the bones of a mouse. But the nest I saw could not have been used by a hawk because hawks do not have young so early in the season. I therefore concluded that these must be owl pellets. Furthermore, the owl was probably a great horned owl, because the other local woodland owls nest in hollow trees. In addition, I found feathers and bones in the area, which indicated to me that this was the nest of a powerful predator. I climbed high into a nearby pine tree so that I could look down inside the nest, and there they were—three fuzzy owlets inside their battered old home.

Great horned owl parents defend their nests fiercely, and it wasn't long before the mother owl came on the scene. She snapped her bill, called repeatedly in a hoarse gurgle, and occasionally hooted while staring at me with her huge yellow eyes. Her actions were meant to frighten me away, but she made no attempt to attack me. Being perched none too solidly on top of that large pine, I was grateful indeed that she didn't consider me a threat.

Two days later, the sky turned dark early in the day as storm clouds gathered from the north. The wind stopped blowing, and in the hushed silence, a sticky wet snow began to fall.

Despite the bad weather, I decided to return to the nest to see how the owlets were faring. I made my way through the forest, pulling my hat and scarf closer to my body as the wind delivered its chill. I arrived at the tree only to find that it was badly damaged from the storm. Tangles of branches lay beneath it in piles of soft snow. Two young owlets were perched safely on some fallen limbs. Where was the third?

I pulled out one branch, then another and another. I kicked some snow aside. Nothing. Then—what was that? A foot? No doubt about it—an owl's foot was sticking out of the snow! I gently brushed the powdery white stuff aside.

The owlet attached to that foot was too weak to stand. It was a soggy, sorry-looking little bundle. It lay on its side, head hunched down between its shoulders like a turtle in its shell. Its stubby wings moved weakly in slow motion, and its bill was partially open in fright as it stared up at me. Only the eyes showed some signs of life. I plucked up the limp little bird and carefully tucked it inside my jacket. I decided there was nothing to do but take it home.

April 21

Revived by the warmth of the wood-burning stove, Bubo stands up in his grass-filled cardboard box, glares at me, and hisses. I dangle a piece of meat in front of him, but he ignores it. As I gently push the meat inside his open bill, he at first remains motionless, then greedily swallows the morsel. Each succeeding piece of meat I offer goes down faster than the one before. As the nourishment revives him, all signs of shyness begin to fade.

Well fed and alert, Bubo stands up tall and clacks his bill as if he's in charge here. His fluffy down has dried, making him look twice as big as before. He spreads his wings and raises the feathers on his back, and he looks larger yet. Then he faces me and continues to clack his bill while rocking from side to side, missing no trick to make himself look as large and menacing as possible. All the while, his eyes do not leave me.

His large yellow eyes are positioned on the front of his flat face, not at the sides as with other birds; his eyelashes are very thick. I remember reading that baby great horned owls are born with pale blue eyes that change to yellow long before the owlet leaves the nest. Where one would expect a nose on a human face, Bubo has a curved bill with a nostril on each side. Most of the bill is hidden by stiff, hairlike feathers.

Bubo is only three to four weeks old. He already weighs about three pounds and will not gain much more weight. Young great horned owls achieve nearly their full weight but not their size by this age. I measure Bubo, and, standing flat on his feet, he is about twelve and a half inches tall. He may grow another seven inches or so by the time he is an adult. I am awed by the thought that his wingspan may grow to fifty-five inches! Right now he hardly extends his wings at all, and his feathers are still short: his tail is a mere stub, and his wing feathers extend less than an inch beyond the quills. But the talons are already well developed, and sharp. As if poking through wool socks, they extend ridiculously far beyond the ends of his toes, which are delicately covered in cream-colored down. Hanging over the legs and extending over both sides, the long, fluffy belly feathers look like a pair of bloomers.

His coat is functional: as long as it remains dry, it helps to keep his body warm. Owlets are covered with a fuzzy white natal down almost from the time they hatch. When they are about three weeks old, this down is replaced by a longer, buff-colored, soft and fluffy secondary down.

Though Bubo looks harmless and cuddly now, he will not always be that way. Great horned owls are known to be fierce, defiant, and untamable.

Bubo is now too old to be brooded, that is, his mother would no longer need to keep him warm with her body if he were in the wild. But as substitute parent, I still have certain chores. And he is not cooperating. He is standing at eye level in his cardboard box in front of me, and whenever I move, he immediately hunches down, spreads his wings, and puffs himself out, rocking furiously from side to side. He hisses and snaps his bill in a rapid series of clacks. His suspicious, gleaming eyes stay fully open and follow my every movement.

In the evening, I cut up a dead mouse from the mousetrap and put a small piece into his

hooked open bill. He clamps down on it, hesitates a second, and then swallows. No matter how gently I withdraw my hand, he is on full alert again and takes on a defensive posture with blazing eyes and snapping bill. Again I place a small piece of meat in his bill and speak to him softly, and the wild look in his eyes disappears.

April 24
After four days of being constantly at my side, Bubo is calmer. After I talk to him in gentle, soothing tones for about two minutes, he begins to smooth his feathers, closes his bill, and pulls in his outstretched wings. But when I make any sudden movement, such as turning the page of a book or lifting a pencil, he comes to full attention and acts as wild as before. So I talk to him again in a lulling whisper, and he calmly closes his eyes.

April 26
Bubo has been here for five days now, and he has become downright tolerant of me. By moving my hand very slowly, I can even reach behind him and scratch the back of his head. But that makes him shake his head, as if he is trying to get rid of a bothersome bug. I scratch there some more, and his feathers feel soft and fuzzy, warm to the touch. When I feel the feathers on his belly, he starts to groom his wings, drawing each feather through his big hooked bill. Then he proceeds to balance on one foot, closes his eyes, and gently scratches the feathers around his eyes with one of the great talons of the other foot. The preening completed, Bubo fluffs himself out and shakes himself violently. Finally, he rises tall on his woolly legs, stretches one wing and his neck, and gently sighs.

April 28

I want to transfer Bubo out of his nest box and onto the arm of the sofa beside me. This is not an easy task, because right now he doesn't want anyone to lay a hand on him. But there is a way. I put on a leather glove and place my hand under his breast. He climbs on, snaps his bill a few times, and clumsily shifts his weight from one foot to the other. Although this is the gentlest way of moving Bubo, I now have the problem of getting my hand back for other uses. It takes a bit of twisting to get him off. He moves around my hand like a lumberjack riding a log on a river drive. Soon he is perched beside me on the arm of the sofa, and, because he wears no diaper, I place a newspaper under him.

The time seems right for a meal, and I have just the thing for Bubo. Bunny, my wife Margaret's cat, has brought in a dead bird—a hermit thrush. I show it to the owlet, but he doesn't seem to recognize it as food. I wonder if his parents would still tear the prey apart for him. Would he accept the bird as food if it were cut up and handed to him in small pieces? I attend to this chore, and the answer to my question is a resounding "yes." After this meal, Bubo smacks his bill in contentment for two or three minutes, drawing his tongue in and out, in and out. He fluffs out and shakes himself, and seeing how snug and cozy he is, I feel happy, too.

After this ritual, he shifts his attention to his environment. Turning his head around ever so slowly—right, left, up, down—he inspects the walls, the floor, the ceiling; then he peers out the window for a while. Next, the wood stove becomes a big attraction, and he excitedly bobs his head up and down and to the side and back. This bobbing action helps him to gain depth perception, view an object from several directions, and get a clearer view of the stove. After a frenzied ten-minute inspection of the whole room, during which he totally ignores me, he makes a decision: he leaps off the sofa and onto the chair. His feet grasp the cloth of the chair, but his heavy body lags behind, so he dangles from a talon or two and weakly flaps his wings. I help him onto the chair and his talons draw a few drops of my blood. Then he bumbles onto the floor, and walks on his oversized feet by hunching down and leaning forward, taking slow, clumsy, purposeful steps while his wings are pulled in tightly. A ballerina he is not. Margaret does not like the floor whitewashed with Bubo's droppings, so I diligently return him to his perch over the newspaper.

May 4
Bubo is beginning to show some hunting instincts. Earlier today he carefully watched a large beetle scurry along the floor, although he did not attack it. Now he is playing hunter by attacking a leaf and a piece of straw from the broom, grasping them in one of his huge taloned feet. He lifts the foot up to his face, and with great care transfers the objects to his bill. He is amazingly persistent and undisturbed by my laughter.

How much will Bubo's natural behavior change because of his association with me? It is not likely that he will hunt like a "real" wild owl as long as he is watched by a human observer. But the instincts to hunt and fly are there within him, and, given the opportunity, he will learn to do both. I intend to make sure he gets that chance.

Thinking About It

1. "I brought it home. Can I keep it?" Words such as these have been spoken many times. When should the answer be *yes* and when should it be *no?*

2. Judging from this diary, do you think a wild owl would make a good house pet? Give evidence from the diary.

3. You've probably heard the expressions "Wise as an owl" or "I don't give a hoot." Think of other expressions about animals. In each case, what is suggested about animal or human behavior?

Another Book by a Naturalist

Feral: Tame Animals Gone Wild by Laurence Pringle. This naturalist describes animals who, unlike Heinrich's owl, have gone from tame to wild.

VIRGINIA HAMILTON

Gram Tut and the Care

Y ou hear that?" Cammy asked Gram Tut.
"Otha Vance is building a hog house. And
asking you to help him."

She thought she heard Gram Tut crow
thinly. But she wasn't sure. Gram was
over there, in the bed by the window. And the
sound was like a rooster from way across the barn-
yard.

Tut didn't turn her head to greet her grand-
child. She didn't move at all.

Cammy walked across the darkened room and
turned on the light above the sink. She tiptoed to
the bed, hopped up on the side rail and leaned
close. Gram Tut's eyes were closed. Already the
smell of the place, of old people, was up her nose.
Cammy smacked a big kiss on her grandmother's
cheek.

"There! I planted it, Gram. Now don't wash

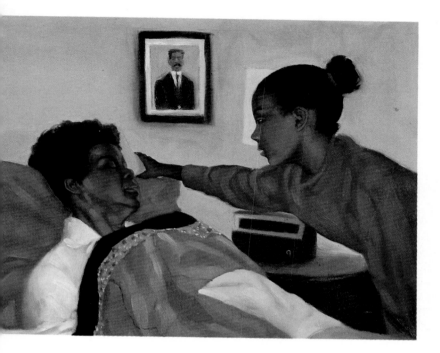

it. Let it grow." Something about her Gram
brought out the best in Cammy.

Tut couldn't wash her own face. "Poor old
thing," Cammy's mama said.

You're not poor anything, Cammy thought,
looking down at her Gram. She touched the lines
of crisscross wrinkles on Gram's cheek. "You're
my Gram and you need me to snuggle your face
once in a while," she said.

Cammy didn't snuggle against Gram now. She
would do that before she left. It always made Gram
cry. But Gram Tut liked her to do that all the
same.

"Gram?" Cammy leaned closer. Gram Tut's
eyes were still closed. "You're not dead yet, are
you?"

There was a long moment in which Cammy
held her breath. But then, Tut gave a grin; said

weakly, "Fooled ya!" and shot her eyes wide open.

It was a rough game that Tut managed to play with Cammy. Pretend dead-as-a-doornail was what Cammy called it. Gram Tut thought that was a riot. She was usually half awake when Cammy came. She would hear her granddaughter tiptoeing in and she would at once play dead.

"Don't tell Maylene," Tut had said. Maylene was Gram Tut's daughter and Cammy's mama. "She doesn't have a fingernail bit of humor in her."

They never played the game when anybody else was around.

Now, Cammy grinned. "Gram," she said, "you didn't fool me. I knew you was here, and always will be, too."

"Expect so, the rate I've been here," murmured Tut.

"Ninety-four years!" squealed Cammy.

"Oh, surely, not that long!" Tut said, softly.

Cammy let it go. "Gram Tut?"

What, honey? Tut's throat moved but she hadn't the strength right then to speak.

"Did you hear what I said? Otha Vance is building hisself a hog house . . ."

Him. Himself, honey. Not hisself, Tut thought. Doesn't Maylene or that school teach you a thing?

"He needs some help, Mister Vance says," Cammy explained. "Me and you could help him, if you want."

Cammy knew better than that. Mr. Vance lived at the Care, also. She knew he wouldn't build a hog house, nor could Gram Tut help him at anything. But it was part of the game, like saying to Gram, "What did you do today?" And Gram Tut saying back, "I'm worn out. I cleaned the whole

A · 124

house," when everybody knew she was mostly bedridden. She had no house now.

"Did you hear what I said, Gram?"

This time, Tut did get the words out before the strength left her completely. She hoarded her energy every morning after breakfast, knowing that Cammy would come see her later. And the child, talking a blue streak.

Tut's dry lips parted, "Tell that old fool he'll never make another pig sty . . . nor wallow in the mud-manure, either," Tut said. Her voice was just above a whisper, getting stronger, now that she had someone to talk to.

"I hate hogs," Cammy told her.

"But you love the sound of spareribs knocking . . . their taste in your mouth," Tut murmured.

"And with sourdough bread, good and hot, with the butter dripping out of it! Ooooh!" moaned Cammy.

"Mom has made her last meal on this earth," Cammy's mama, Maylene, had said one day about Gram Tut.

They all missed Gram Tut's cooking. When it first happened that she no longer could cook, before the Care, she would sit in the kitchen. Maylene would do the cooking with Tut at her elbow. "Put a little ketsup in with the chicken and flour. You don't need to fry it, Maylene. Do as I say," Tut would tell her. "Just stick it in the oven with a little vinegar and honey. You never do listen to what I tell you."

Her mama had to do it her way. Said the idea of ketsup and vinegar made her want to upchuck. She fried everything. The chicken she made, though, was all right. But greasy.

Not as good as my Gram doing it, herself, in

the oven, Cammy thought now. Not never that good, yummy-yum.

"I always stir a little love and kisses into my food," Gram said.

Oh, Gram! "Maybe you can make us something good-tasting for Christmas," sighed Cammy. And then: "You asleep?" Tut went in and out of sleep easily. Her mouth lay slack, drawn to one side of her face.

"That's no kind a Christmas dinner— chicken," Tut said, suddenly wide awake. She had been thinking about her summer curtains. Better had get them up, and the screens in, too. Get up just after dawn, before I start in baking pies. What month is it? Where am I? she thought. Oh.

It surprised Cammy when Gram's voice became so young and fresh.

"You want turkey and duck . . . for Christmas, like in the old times," Tut said. She remembered her Grandfather Sam shooting fox. Pretty little things.

"Truly, Gram? Will you come home when it's Christmas and make it for us?" Cammy asked, all eagerness, forgetting that Gram was old and might not live that long.

"Child . . . you wear me out . . . in five minutes. I swept the grass . . . no . . . I swept the porch. I mean . . . the whole house. What more . . . where is Thy light!" Gram's voice quavered on the last words.

"Gram," Cammy said. She knew her Gram was helped out of bed twice a day for lunch and for dinner. She watched Gram Tut closely.

Sometimes, Gram's mind took a wrong turn, Maylene said.

Tut closed her eyes and opened them. Her

gaze wandered, found the portrait of her husband, Emmet, high up on the wall.

Gramper Em-un-Ems, Cammy had called him when she was five or six. Tut had thought that was so cute.

Now Tut was whispering at the portrait. Cammy thought she was speaking to her. "Don't talk, Gram, 'cause it wears you out. Just listen. I was telling you that Mister Vance wants your help. Hear him outside?" Cammy went on. "His chair squeaking? I think he's coming in now. Gram! Shall I let him come in?"

"Does he have his . . . pajama bottoms still on?" Tut said. Her voice had wheezed from her chest. She turned her eyes toward Cammy. She could turn her head sometimes. But she didn't then.

"Sure he has them on. They don't let him walk around silly," Cammy said.

"They say he takes his night clothes off all in the hallway," said Tut.

Cammy knew that had happened a month ago and hadn't happened since or she would've heard. Gram lost plenty of time. She could speed it up, though, when she felt like it.

"Let him on in," Tut said. "Mebbe he knows me today."

Cammy went to the door and directed Otha

Vance in. She spoke grandly but in a soft voice so as not to alert the nurses. "My Gram will see you now, kind sir."

Otha Vance looked Cammy up and down, but didn't answer a word. He rolled in. He was a sagging, pale little man in a wide-brimmed farmer's straw hat, surrounded by his wheelchair. He had moist, beady eyes and no hair to speak of under the hat. He was kept in the chair by a sash around his waist attached to a harness across his shoulders. The harness and sash were tied together at the back of the chair.

Otha seemed to shrink farther into the chair each time Cammy saw him. He had stopped beside Gram's sink to take in her "home." He looked over at the television at the foot of the bed. It was tuned to a talk show. He gazed at the bed crank to judge Gram's condition today. The top of the bed was raised, an aid to keeping her lungs free of fluid.

"Got a cold?" he hollered. He never could speak softly. He didn't get an answer, either. He didn't expect any, and didn't listen, anyhow. He took in the bed last, with Cammy standing there on the railing. Her neck was craned around to watch him. She eyed him suspiciously.

Swiftly, Otha rolled up behind her and pinched her waist.

"Ouch! You old—I knew you were going to do that!" He had been so fast. Cammy made a spitball. Otha saw her mouth working and raised his hand to her. She parted her mouth just so he could see the spit a minute. He dropped his hand at that.

I'm eleven, Cammy thought. I know better than to use a spitball on an old farmer in a wheelchair. But he don't know I know! Mom would whip my daylights out for doing something like that. Don't know what Andrew would do to me.

Andrew was Cammy's big brother. She was usually in his charge, when he could find her. He never told when she slipped off. It was his fault anyway, for not watching her closely enough. If he told their mama she'd run off, he'd have to admit he'd go looking for her only about half the time.

Andrew was sixteen and hard as nails, people thought. But Cammy knew better. Maylene had been warned by her own sister, Effie Lee, that Andrew could be a drinker. Cammy never ever told on him, either.

Otha gave Cammy one of his blind kind of looks, although he wasn't near blind. He wore glasses that were rimless and always so dirty, he might as well have been blind. He would fall down when he tried to stand on his feet. That was the reason he was tied in the chair. And he was too feeble to live alone any longer in his huge farmhouse. He'd fallen too often and couldn't get up by himself. His children moved him to the Care home.

"Got sixteen cent?" he was asking Tut.

"What for, Otha?" she said. "You forget how to say good morning to me?"

"Gram. It's after four o'clock in the afternoon, goodness sakes," Cammy told her.

"To get a bus so's I can go home," Otha said. "I'll give you a dollar if you call the law."

"What for?" asked Gram, breathless a moment.

"For to arrest that boy of mine. Putting me in here," Otha told her.

"There's no bus," Cammy cut in. "They don't run the bus hardly, least, not to your house. Anyways, your house is been sold."

"You better get outta here, little girl," he said.

"Nurse! Nurse! The kid is messin' around!"

"Hush up, Otha," Gram said.

"Oh, be quiet! Don't see why everybody's so cranky," he said. "The wife's stayed away all day. Mad at me, too." He looked glum.

"He's forgot his Betty has passed," Maylene had told Cammy.

Her mama also said that it was weird the way Otha "fitted to his gravity," was the way she put it. Without warning, he would drop things and fall in a heap. Cammy had seen him standing in the door of his "home" once, that being what they called their rooms at the Care. Most residents had a "home" all to themselves. Some few men shared their "homes" in big, double rooms. But one time, somehow Otha blew himself forward like out of a cannon. He'd shot himself across the hall. His head hit the railing the elders held to when they walked, when they could walk, and which they pulled themselves along when they were in wheelchairs.

It hadn't hurt Otha. "Farmer," Maylene had said, "hard-headed as he can be."

Gram said, quietly, with her eyes closed, "So, Otha . . . what you . . . up to?"

"He's building a hog hut, I told you," Cammy said.

"Oh, will you be quiet?" Otha said. "I'm talking to your mother."

"No, you're not!" Cammy and Gram said almost at the same time.

Cammy squealed with laughter, just as Lilac Rose, the best attendant on the wing, stopped to study the three of them.

"Party time," she said, coming in to check on Gram Tut. "Hello there, Miz Tut," she said. "How's my favorite lady this afternoon?" She lifted the blanket and looked and felt under Tut to see if she was still "comfortable," was the way she put it. That meant dry, Cammy knew. Cammy turned her face away from what Lilac was doing. At the same time, she blocked Otha's view.

Gram Tut peered at Lilac Rose. They looked deeply of one another. Tut said not a word. Lilac Rose worked silently.

"Hi, Lilac, I love you," Cammy said, sweetly.

Lilac smiled. "Hi, baby. I love you, too," she answered.

"Don't tell on me, please?" Cammy pleaded.

"Huh. Haven't seen nobody," Lilac said, breezily. "Haven't heard nothing."

Anybody. Goodness. Haven't heard anything. Lordy, Tut thought.

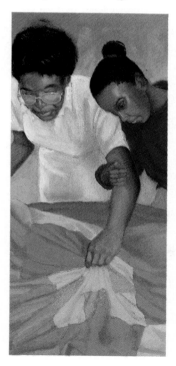

"Thank you, Lilac," Cammy whispered. She placed her cheek on the brown coolness of Lilac's arm as Lilac took care of Gram. Lilac Rose never minded her and never told on her to a soul.

"I'm goin' tell," Otha said, peering around Cammy's back. "Kid!"

"Oh, Otha, get out of here! Don't always be so rotten," Lilac said. "Miz Tut likes having her grandbaby come visit."

"Well, I will, too, tell," Otha said. "There's nobody come to see me!"

"So whose fault is that?" asked Lilac Rose.

Otha wouldn't say. Perhaps he hadn't heard. For he backed his chair carefully to the door. All at once, he shot through the opening and across the hall. He held his feet high off the floor as the wheels spun in reverse. He hit the railing with full force. And gave out a hog call that Cammy could admire. It wasn't ear-splitting, though, like the kind the young hog callers could do at the county fair.

There was a thud as, quite by accident, the chair with Otha fell over on its side from the impact. The noise in the cool, dim hallway caused a stir, and cries of, "Help! Nurse! Somebody help me!"—up and down the wing.

"Oh, oh," Lilac said, under her breath. She went on about her business with Gram. She changed Tut's bed gown and turned her on her side facing the door. Then she gave a glance toward the hallway. "Better beat it, Cammy," she said. "In a few minutes, I've got to get your Gram up for supper, too."

Miss Mimi across the hall came wheeling out of her home. She peeked out to see if Otha was all right. Her hair was rolled in a fresh pompadour. Lipstick and rouge prettied her face. She gave Otha the once-over, as if he were some alien, iron bug wiggling on its side. Then, she wheeled on by him down the hall. "I'm coming girls, don't fret," she called.

Tut sighed, said to the air, "We take care of . . . our own, don't we?"

The nurse's station wasn't far up at the center of long corridors to the three wings. In a minute, ladies in white would be all over the place, Cammy thought. She said so to Lilac. "But shouldn't you go pick Mister Vance up?"

Go pick *up* Mister Vance, honey. Maylene hasn't taught you a thing, Tut was thinking.

"Honey, it'll take two at least to get him and that chair up off the floor," Lilac said, dryly. "If I try to move him, they'll say I oughtn't've. Shoulda waited for a nurse. Next thing, they'll turn around and yell at me for not helping him."

Still, Cammy thought Lilac should have gone to help him. She couldn't be seen out there to go, herself. He could have been hurt bad.

Lilac had started combing Gram's hair as best she could. Cammy watched. "One day, I comb it while she's lying like this," said Lilac. "Next time, I comb it after she's in the chair."

Now they heard feet scurrying.

"That way, in a couple of times, I get most of it done," Lilac went on.

Otha began shouting, "Somebody! Somebody!"

"All right, Otha, we're coming," somebody called.

"Better had fade away, honey," said Lilac.

"Can't I stay? I could hide under the bed," Cammy whispered, her eyes darting. "I could say my mama just went to the restroom, if anybody sees me."

"It could be a pool nurse," Cammy added.

The pool nurses came in a rotation from the nearby hospitals. "They wouldn't know who I was."

"It's not the weekend," Lilac said. "Best you scoot."

Cammy waited by the sink. Ida, the nurse, and Dave, the assistant, were bent over Otha, examining him and asking him questions. Soon they had him upright in his chair and in his room. Otha shouted one second and moaned the next, as they closed the door.

Cammy went back to Gram, climbed up on the railing and said a hurried good-bye. "See you tomorrow," she said. She snuggled Gram's face.

Don't go! Tut thought. Need you to climb back up with my curtains.

"Gram? I love you best!" Cammy whispered into Gram's ear. More than Mama? she thought. Well, just as much.

"Don't go!" Gram Tut wailed.

"Now, now," Lilac soothed. "Shhh. Shhh, darlin'."

"Don't go." The whole night is coming. Tut could feel it creeping up on her. Big tears slid down her face.

"Oh, now, Miz Tut, everything's going to be fine," said Lilac. "I'm here and you'll soon be up in your chair, ready for your good supper."

Cammy was out of the room. She shut down her insides against Gram Tut's crying. And slipped away toward the big glass door at the end of the hall.

Glad it's Lilac with Gram, she thought. Shameful that my sorry cousins don't come to visit her some. Patty Ann. Richie. Glad the Care's not a bad place, though, like some they say are.

Pulling it all

TOGETHER

1. You are Cammy in "Gram Tut and the Care." How is Gram Tut a deciding factor in your life? Explain.

2. Each selection in this book is about something that really matters to someone and the decisions that come from caring so much. How do the things the characters value compare to the things you value? Your answer could be the opening paragraph of your own autobiography.

3. Now it's *your* turn to make some decisions. If you were putting together a book for seventh-graders, which of the selections in this book would you include? What would you add?

BOOKS to ENJOY

Cave Under the City
by Harry Mazer
Harper, 1986
Twelve-year-old Tolly and his
younger brother flee to the streets
when their father leaves home in
search of work and their mother becomes ill. The story takes place in the
1930s, but it could have happened
today.

Sports Pages
by Arnold Adoff
Harper, 1986
Soccer, football, gymnastics, wres-
tling, track, baseball, and more—this
collection of poems moves from sport
to sport, showing the moods and determination of athletes.

If This Is Love, I'll Take Spaghetti
by Ellen Conford
Scholastic, 1983
Have you wanted to meet a rock star?
Have you waited for a special phone
call? Have you tried to cover up your
shyness? Read nine stories about teen-
agers who decide what really matters.

Dogsong
by Gary Paulsen
Bradbury, 1985
A young Eskimo sets out alone on a journey on dogsled to discover himself and his roots. But he discovers that he is not alone in the wilderness.

Circus Dreams
by Kathleen Cushman and Montana Miller
Little, Brown, 1990
At eighteen, Montana Miller goes to France to become a trapeze artist. Her schedule is tough, but the rewards make it a wonderful year.

Baseball in April
by Gary Soto
Harcourt, 1990
In these stories, young people display the desires, fears, victories, and defeats that are all part of growing up. The characters make decisions—not all of them wise—that help direct their lives.

Beauty: A Retelling of the Story of Beauty and the Beast
by Robin McKinley
Harper, 1978
Her father made a promise. Now *she* has to fulfill it. She couldn't possibly fall in love in the process. Or could she?

Literary Terms

Autobiography An autobiography is the story of a real person's life told by that person. It is written from the first-person point of view and may tell all or only part of the person's life. In "And the Dogs Could Teach Me," Gary Paulsen tells of an experience that changed his life.

Characterization Authors develop characters through speech, actions, and thoughts. In "If This Is Love, I'll Take Spaghetti," you learn about Jamie's weight problem through her conversations with Judy and her family. From her refusal to eat some of the hero sandwich, you learn that she will continue the diet. From Jamie's thoughts, you learn that she doesn't want to hate herself anymore; she won't lose weight for anyone except herself.

Diary A diary is a written account of events in a real person's life and of how that person thinks and feels about the events. Usually entries are made daily. "Nature's Notebook" is from a book that is written in a diary format.

Figurative Language In figurative language, words take on meanings beyond the ordinary literal ones. Two things that are unlike may be compared to provide a vivid picture. In "Oranges," the poet describes candies as "tiered like bleachers." A comparison using the word *like* or the word *as* is called a simile.

In "Black Hair," the poet talks of crouching "before an altar of worn baseball cards," showing how much he worshiped the great baseball players. This kind of comparison is called a metaphor. In a metaphor the comparison is not directly stated.

Irony Irony is a contrast between what appears to be and what really is. The irony comes in the ending of *The Necklace* when Mathilde makes an unexpected discovery about the piece of jewelry she had borrowed years before from her friend.

Plot: Conflict and Resolution Plot is a series of events selected by the author to present and resolve some conflict. The events lead to a turning point in the story, and the conflict is resolved in the conclusion. In "Seventh Grade," there is conflict when Victor tries to attract Teresa, a turning point as Victor pretends to speak French and risks looking foolish, and a resolution in the happy ending.

Setting The setting is the time and place of the events in a story. What is important about the setting varies from selection to selection. For example, in "Seventh Grade" the school setting at the beginning of a new year is important, not the city or the year.

Symbol A symbol is a person, place, event, or object that has a meaning in itself but suggests other meanings as well. In "MVP," the key is a symbol to Joan Benoit that she is growing up.

GLOSSARY

Vocabulary from your selections

ad mon ish (ad mon′ish), *v.t.* **1** advise against something; warn: *admonish a person of danger.* **2** scold gently; reprove: *admonish a student for careless work.* **3** urge strongly; advise earnestly.

ad o les cence (ad′l es′ns), *n.* **1** growth from childhood to adulthood. **2** youth.

ad ver si ty (ad vėr′sə tē), *n., pl.* **-ties.** condition of being in unfavorable circumstances.

al le vi ate (ə lē′vē āt), *v.t.,* **-at ed, -at ing.** **1** make easier to endure (suffering of the body or mind); relieve; mitigate: *Heat often alleviates pain.* **2** lessen or lighten; diminish.

am bro sia (am brō′zhə), *n.* **1** (in Greek and Roman myths) the food of the gods. **2** anything especially delightful to taste or smell.

am bro sial (am brō′zhəl), *adj.* like ambrosia; very fragrant or delicious.

a wak en ing (ə wā′kə ning), *n.* a waking up; arousing. —*adj.* arousing.

ban dit (ban′dit), *n., pl.* **ban dits, ban dit ti** (ban dit′ē). **1** person who robs, especially one of a gang of robbers; brigand. **2** any outlaw.

bed rid den (bed′rid′n), *adj.* confined to bed for a long time because of sickness or weakness.

be grudge (bi gruj′), *v.t.,* **-grudged, -grudg ing.** be reluctant to give or allow (something); grudge.

binge (binj), *n.* INFORMAL. **1** a drunken spree. **2** a bout or spree of indulgence in anything.

blus ter (blus′tər), *v.i.* **1** storm noisily; blow violently: *The wind blustered around the house.* **2** talk noisily and violently: *They were very excited and angry, and blustered for a while.* —*v.t.* **1** do or say noisily and violently. **2** make or get by blustering.

ca ma ra der ie (kä′mə rä′dər ē), *n.* friendliness and loyalty among comrades; comradeship.

cap tiv i ty (kap tiv′ə tē), *n., pl.* **-ties.** **1** condition of being in prison. **2** condition of being held against one's will.

cat e chism (kat′ə kiz′əm), *n.* book of questions and answers about religion, used for teaching religious doctrine.

chafe (chāf), *v.,* **chafed, chaf ing.** —*v.i.* **1** become worn away by rubbing. **2** become irritated by rubbing. **3** become angry: *I chafed under their teasing.*

cha grin (shə grin´), *n.* a feeling of disappointment, failure, or humiliation. —*v.t.* cause to feel chagrin.

com pla cent (kəm plā´snt), *adj.* pleased with oneself or what one has; self-satisfied.

con sti tute (kon´stə tüt, kon´stə tyüt), *v.t.*, **-tut ed, -tut ing.** make up; form; comprise: *Seven days constitute a week.*

con sul ta tion (kon´səl tā´shən), *n.* **1** act of consulting; seeking information or advice. **2** a meeting to exchange ideas or talk things over; conference.

con ten tion (kən ten´shən), *n.* **1** statement or point that one has argued for; statement maintained as true. **2** an arguing; quarreling: *Contention has no place in the classroom.* **3** argument; dispute; quarrel. **4** struggle; contest; competition.

de ter mi na tion (di tèr´mə nā´shən), *n.* great firmness in carrying out a purpose; fixed purpose: *My determination was not weakened by the misfortune.*

dis dain (dis dān´), *v.t.* think unworthy of oneself or one's notice; regard or treat with contempt; scorn. —*n.* a disdaining; feeling of scorn.

doc ile (dos´əl; *British* dō´sīl, dos´īl), *adj.* easily managed or trained; obedient.

dow ry (dou´rē), *n., pl.* **-ries.** money or property that a woman brings to the man she marries.

dry (drī), *adj.*, **dri er, dri est. 1** not wet; not moist: *dry clothes.* **2** having little or no rain: *a dry climate.* **3** having little or no natural or ordinary moisture: *a dry tongue.* **4** showing no feeling; cold or restrained: *a dry answer.* **5** humorous in an unemotional or somewhat sarcastic way: *dry humor.* **6** not interesting; dull: *a dry subject.*

dry ly (drī´lē), *adv.* in a dry manner. Also **drily.**

e lec tive (i lek´tiv), *adj.* **1** chosen by an election: *Senators are elective officials.* **2** open to choice; not required; optional: *Spanish is an elective subject in many high schools.* —*n.* subject or course of study which may be taken, but is not required.

ex alt (eg zôlt´), *v.t.* **1** make high in rank, honor, power, character, or quality; elevate. **2** fill with pride, joy, or noble feeling. **3** praise; honor; glorify.

ex al ta tion (eg´zôl tā´shən), *n.* **1** an exalting. **2** a being exalted. **3** elation of mind or feeling; rapture.

fee ble (fē´bəl), *adj.*, **-bler, -blest. 1** lacking strength; weak; frail. **2** lacking in energy or force.

gorge (gôrj), *n., v.*, **gorged, gorg ing.** —*n.* **1** a deep, narrow valley, usually steep and rocky, especially one with a stream. **2** contents of a stomach. —*v.i.* eat greedily until full. —*v.t.* **1** stuff with food: *He gorged himself with cake at the party.* **2** fill full.

ham let (ham´lit), *n.* a small village; little group of houses in the country.

hoard (hôrd, hōrd), *v.t., v.i.* save and store away (money, goods, etc.) for preservation or future use: *A squirrel hoards nuts for the winter.*

i ron i cal (ī ron´ə kəl), *adj.* **1** expressing one thing and meaning the opposite. **2** contrary to what would naturally be expected. —**i ron´i cal ly,** *adv.*

a hat	**oi** oil
ā age	**ou** out
ä far	**u** cup
e let	**ú** put
ē equal	**ü** rule
ėr term	
i it	**ch** child
ī ice	**ng** long
o hot	**sh** she
ō open	**th** thin
ô order	**ᴛʜ** then
	zh measure

ə = { a in about
e in taken
i in pencil
o in lemon
u in circus

< = derived from

hamlet

kale (def. 1)

kale (kāl), *n.* **1** species of cole having loose, curled leaves. Kale looks somewhat like spinach. **2** its leaves, eaten as a vegetable.

ken nel (ken′l), *n.* house for a dog or dogs.

len ien cy (lē′nyən sē, lē′nē ən sē), *n.* lenient quality; mildness; gentleness; mercy.

len ient (lē′nyənt, lē′nē ənt), *adj.* mild or gentle.

lime light (līm′līt′), *n.* **1** an intense white light produced by heating a piece of lime in a flame, formerly used in a theater to light up certain persons or objects on the stage. **2** center of public attention and interest.

lobe (lōb), *n.* a rounded projecting part. The brain, liver, etc., are divided into lobes. The lobe of the ear is the lower rounded end.

mel o dra ma (mel′ə drä′mə, mel′ə dram′ə), *n.* a sensational drama with exaggerated appeal to the emotions and, usually, a happy ending.

mim e o graph (mim′ē ə graf), *n.* machine for making copies of written or typewritten material. —*v.t.* make (copies) with a mimeograph.

moon (mün), *n.* a heavenly body that revolves around the earth. —*v.i.* wander about or gaze idly or dreamily. —*v.t.* spend (time) idly.

muz zle (muz′əl), *n.* **1** the projecting part of the head of an animal, including the nose, mouth, and jaws; snout. **2** cover or cage of straps or wires to put over an animal's head or mouth to keep it from biting or eating.

nat ur al ist (nach′ər ə list), *n.* person who makes a study of living organisms, especially in their native habitats; zoologist, botanist, etc.

neu tral ize (nü′trə līz, nyü′trə līz), *v.t.,* **-ized, -iz ing.** **1** make chemically or electrically neutral. **2** make of no effect by some opposite force; counterbalance.

notch (noch), *n.* a V-shaped nick or cut made in an edge or on a curving surface. —*v.t.* make a notch or notches in.

op er a (op′ər ə), *n.* play in which music is an essential and prominent part, featuring arias, choruses, etc., with orchestral accompaniment.

owl et (ou′lit), *n.* **1** a young owl. **2** a small owl.

owlet (def. 1)

pas sion (pash′ən), *n.* **1** a very strong or violent feeling or emotion, such as great hate and fear. **2** a very strong liking: *She has a passion for music.* **3** object of such a strong liking: *Music is her passion.*

pen chant (pen′chənt), *n.* a strong taste or liking; inclination: *a penchant for taking long walks.*

pos ture (pos′chər), *n., v.,* **-tured, -tur ing.** —*n.* position of the body; way of holding the body. —*v.i.* **1** take a certain posture: *The dancer postured before the mirror, bending and twisting her body.* **2** pose for effect.

pred a tor (pred′ə tər), *n.* animal or person that is predatory.

pred a to ry (pred′ə tôr′ē, pred′ə tōr′ē), *adj.* living by preying upon other animals. Hawks and owls are predatory birds.

pre mo ni tion (prē′mə nish′ən, prem′ə nish′ən), *n.* notification or warning of what is to come; forewarning: *a vague premonition of disaster.*

promissory note, a written promise to pay a stated sum of money to a certain person at a certain time.

pros per ous (pros′pər əs), *adj.* **1** doing well; prospering; successful. **2** favorable; helpful.

pul sate (pul′sāt), *v.i.,* **-sat ed, -sat ing. 1** expand and contract rhythmically, as the heart or an artery; beat; throb. **2** vibrate; quiver.

quiv er (kwiv′ər), *v.i.* shake with a slight but rapid motion; shiver; tremble.

re proach (ri prōch′), *n.* **1** blame or censure. **2** expression of blame, censure, or disapproval. —*v.t.* blame or censure; upbraid.

schol ar (skol′ər), *n.* a learned person; person having much knowledge.

scowl (skoul), *v.i.* **1** look angry or sullen by lowering the eyebrows; frown. **2** have a gloomy or threatening aspect. —*n.* an angry, sullen look; frown.

scrab ble (skrab′əl), *v.,* **-bled, -bling,** *n.* —*v.i.* scratch or scrape about with hands, claws, etc.; scramble. —*n.* a scraping; scramble.

soothe (süᴛʜ), *v.,* **soothed, sooth ing.** —*v.t.* **1** quiet; calm; comfort: *The mother soothed the crying child.* **2** make less painful; relieve; ease. —*v.i.* have or exercise a soothing influence.

tap es try (tap′ə strē), *n., pl.* **-tries.** fabric with pictures or designs woven in it, used to hang on walls, cover furniture, etc.

tol er ant (tol′ər ənt), *adj.* willing to let other people do as they think best; willing to endure beliefs and actions of which one does not approve.

tran si tion (tran zish′ən), *n.* a change or passing from one condition, place, thing, activity, topic, etc., to another.

u sur er (yü′zhər ər), *n.* person who lends money at an extremely high or unlawful rate of interest.

ves ti bule (ves′tə byül), *n.* passage or hall between the outer door and the inside of a building.

vin di cate (vin′də kāt), *v.t.,* **-cat ed, -cat ing. 1** clear from suspicion, dishonor, a hint or charge of wrongdoing, etc. **2** defend successfully against opposition; uphold; justify.

wince (wins), *v.,* **winced, winc ing,** *n.* —*v.i.* draw back suddenly; flinch slightly: *I winced when the dentist's drill touched my tooth.* —*n.* act of wincing.

wrest (rest), *v.t.* twist, pull, or tear away with force; wrench away: *She wrested the knife from her attacker.*

zo ol o gist (zō ol′ə jist), *n.* an expert in zoology.
zo ol o gy (zō ol′ə jē), *n.* branch of biology that deals with animals and animal life.

a hat	oi oil
ā age	ou out
ä far	u cup
e let	u̇ put
ē equal	ü rule
ėr term	
i it	ch child
ī ice	ng long
o hot	sh she
ō open	th thin
ô order	ᴛʜ then
	zh measure

ə = { a in about
e in taken
i in pencil
o in lemon
u in circus

< = derived from

tapestry

Acknowledgments

Text

Page 6: "Seventh Grade" from *Baseball in April*, copyright © 1990 by Gary Soto, reprinted by permission of Harcourt Brace Jovanovich, Inc.

Page 16: "Oranges" reprinted from *Black Hair* by Gary Soto, by permission of the University of Pittsburgh Press. © 1985 by Gary Soto.

Page 18: "The Gymnast" reprinted from *A Summer Life* by Gary Soto. Copyright © 1990 by University Press of New England. By permission of University Press of New England.

Page 24: "Black Hair" reprinted from *Black Hair* by Gary Soto, by permission of the University of Pittsburgh Press. © 1985 by Gary Soto.

Page 26: "On Sports and Young Love," by Gary Soto. Copyright © by Gary Soto, 1991.

Page 30: "And the Dogs Could Teach Me" reprinted with permission of Bradbury Press, an affiliate of Macmillan, Inc. from *Woodsong* by Gary Paulsen. Copyright © 1990 by Gary Paulsen.

Page 42: "Opera, Karate, and Bandits," text pp. 52–61 from *The Land I Lost* by Huynh Quang Nhuong. Text copyright © 1982 by Huynh Quang Nhuong. Reprinted by permission of HarperCollins Publishers.

Page 52: "MVP" from *Running Tide* by Joan Benoit. Copyright © 1987 by Joan Benoit Samuelson. Reprinted by permission of Alfred A. Knopf, Inc.

Page 68: "If This Is Love, I'll Take Spaghetti" reprinted with permission of Four Winds Press, an imprint of Macmillan Publishing Company from *If This Is Love, I'll Take Spaghetti* by Ellen Conford. Text copyright © 1983 by Ellen Conford.

Page 88: "The Necklace" by Guy de Maupassant. Adapted by Earl J. Dias. From *Plays*, April 1987. Reprinted by permission of Plays, Inc. Publishers.

Page 108: "Nature's Notebook" from *An Owl in the House: A Naturalist's Diary* by Bernd Heinrich. Adapted by Alice Calaprice. Text adaptation copyright © 1990 by Alice Calaprice. By permission of Little, Brown and Company.

Page 122: "Gram Tut and the Care" from *Cousins* by Virginia Hamilton, copyright © 1990 by Virginia Hamilton. Reprinted by permission of Philomel Books.

Artists

Seth Jaben, Cover, 3, 4–5, 135, 136, 138, 140
José Ortega, 6–29
Wayne McLaughlin, 30–41
Jeffrey Smith, 42–51
Lilla Rogers, 68–87
Anita Kunz, 88–107
James Ransome, 122–133

Photographs

Page 27: Courtesy of Carolyn Soto
Pages 52, 56, 61, 65, 67, 121: Susan Friedman
Page 108: Wayne Lankinen/Bruce Coleman, Inc.
Page 112: Timothy O'Keefe/Bruce Coleman, Inc.
Page 117: Brian Parker/Tom Stack & Associates

Glossary

The contents of the Glossary entries in this book have been adapted from *Advanced Dictionary*, Copyright © 1988 Scott, Foresman and Company.
Page 141: Don & Pat Valenti
Page 142 (top): E. R. Degginger/Earth Scenes
Page 142 (bottom): Craig K. Lorenz/Photo Researchers
Page 143: The William Morris Gallery, London
Unless otherwise acknowledged, all photographs are the property of Scott Foresman.

Illustrations owned and copyrighted by the illustrator.